THE COTTAGES OF BRITAIN

A HERITAGE OF COUNTRY LIFE

PHILIPPA DRURY

PARKGATE
BOOKS

THE COTTAGES OF BRITAIN

A HERITAGE OF COUNTRY LIFE

First Published in Great Britain in 1997
by Parkgate Books Ltd, London House, Great Eastern Wharf,
London SW11 4NQ

Copyright © Parkgate Books Ltd 1997

Text copyright © Elizabeth Drury and Philippa Lewis 1997

British Library Cataloguing in Publication Data:
A CIP catalogue record for this book is available from the British Library.

ISBN 1- 85585 - 342 - 6

Designed by Paul Vater at Sugar Free
Printed and bound in Italy

CONTENTS

LIST OF COLOUR ILLUSTRATIONS

FOREWORD

'The thatched cottage stood beside the road at one end of a long narrow garden, enclosed from the highway by a hedge of elder. At the back there was a ditch and mound with elm-trees, and green meadows beyond. A few poles used to lean against the thatch, their tops rising above the ridge, and close by was a stack of thorn fagots. In the garden three or four aged and moss-grown apple trees stood among the little plots of potatoes, and as many plum-trees in the elder hedge. One tall pear-tree with scored bark grew near the end of the cottage; it bore a large crop of pears, which were often admired by the people who came along the road, but were really hard and woody. As a child he played in the ditch and hedge, or crept through into the meadow and searched in the spring for violets to offer to the passers-by; or he swung on the gate in the lane and held it open for the farmers in their gigs, in hope of a half-penny.'

This is a description of the British countryside in the early years of the nineteenth century and of a cottage that was home to a farm labourer all his life: a cottage by the wayside, with its own small piece of land. The writer was Richard Jefferies, who had a deep understanding of country places and country people, and a feeling of regret at the passing of all that he knew and loved.

Many of the illustrations in this book, of works by Helen Allingham, Myles Birket Foster and other distinguished Victorian painters, are imbued with a similar sentimental attachment to the past. To them, the cottages were precious relics of former times, altered and adapted by one generation after another of peace-loving folk. As Washington Irving wrote, 'the commonplace of yesterday becomes the poetry of today', with the passage of time; 'the old life becomes ever more and more attractive as it slips away from us, and we watch it disappear with regretful and kindly eyes.'

CHAPTER 1
The Cottage in the Landscape

Behold the cot! where thrives the industrious swain,
Source of his pride, his pleasure, and his gain;
Screen'd from the winter's wind, the sun's last ray
Smiles on the window, and prolongs the day:
Projecting thatch the woodbine's branches stop,
And turn their blossoms to the casement's top:
All need requires is in that cot contained,
And much that taste untaught and unrestrained
Surveys delighted.

George Crabbe

'There is not a more beautiful sight in the world than that of our English cottages', wrote William Howitt in the early years of Queen Victoria's reign. 'On the edges of the forests, in quiet hamlets and sweet woody valleys, the little grey-thatched cottages, with their gardens and old orchards, their rows of beehives, and their porches clustered with jasmines and roses, stand':

Hundreds of huts
All hidden in a sylvan gloom,— some perched
On verdant slopes from the low coppice cleared;
Some in deep dingles, secret as the nest
Of Robin Redbreast, built amongst the roots
Of pine, on whose tall top the throstle sings.

Left: A farm cottage with thatched outbuildings, set in a peaceful summer landscape, with sheep grazing in the foreground.

Left: A view in Kent of a group of estate cottages. Among the trees in the distance is a glimpse of a large house.

Right: The Old Malt House, Brook, Surrey, painted by Helen Allingham. Like the mill and the inn, the malt house was much visited by the cottagers. This one is situated on the edge of the village and well below the level of the lane.

In lyrical vein, he was describing cottages as features in the landscape. Most would have been rebuilt, or repaired and adapted, over the years, and belonged to no particular time or style. They grew and dwindled with their inmates. 'There is nothing obtrusive about the old cottages', wrote the American Washington Irving. 'They do not dominate the landscape, but are content to be part of it, and to pass unnoticed unless one looks specially for their homely beauties.' Villages and hamlets are sometimes close together, sometimes more widely spread, but in England are seldom more than a mile or two apart. 'They have gathered few legends beyond those which time has written on the walls in weather stains and grey lichen.'

'Such places have no history at all, their life has not been set in the public eye, and they have always been so wrapt up in their own affairs, that they have never noticed how times is passing, and so they have brought down into the life of to-day the traditions of two or three hundred years ago,' wrote Stewart Dick.

Left: A cottage near Heathfield in Sussex.

✠ ❉

A farm at Simonsbury, Dorset.

'The lovely cottage in the guardian nook
. . . with its own dear brook,
Its own pasture, almost its own sky.'
William Wordsworth

'In one respect the old cottages are like old ballads', he wrote:

> we have no idea who their authors were. They belong to
> the countryside, and seem just to have grown there, tinged
> and coloured by all the local influences of soil and climate.
> Their architect was the village carpenter, for builder and
> carpenter were the same, when wood was the chief material
> employed. Tradition was his school, the methods handed
> down from father to son were his only methods, but he
> displayed intelligence and ingenuity in adapting them to the
> special requirements of the moment. For it is a
> characteristic of the old life that each little community is
> complete in itself, solving its own problems without
> assistance or advice from the outside. It was a narrow and a
> parochial life perhaps, but it was independent.

In *Our Village*, Mary Russell Mitford portrayed 'a little village far in the country; a small neighbourhood, not of fine mansions finely peopled, but of cottages and cottage-like houses.' Her own village was Three Mile Cross in Berkshire, as delightful a place as was to be found in the first half of the nineteenth century. At the heart of it was the common:

> the right side fringed by hedge-rows and trees, with cottages
> and farm-houses irregularly placed, and terminated by a
> double avenue of noble oaks; the left, prettier still, dappled
> by bright pools of water, and islands of cottages and
> cottage-gardens, and sinking gradually down to cornfields
> and meadows.

Cottages encircling a green had developed from a scattering of huts put up in

Left: A. R. Quinton's watercolour of cottages in a by-lane at Houghton in Sussex. Houghton Forest was a region of dense woodland which supplied plentiful timber for the framing of cottages such as these. The village lies in the shade of Bury Hill, just beneath the Downs.

Right: The village street of Carhampton in Somerset. The medieval church tower is the prominent feature of the view. Many villages began as a group of cottages clustering round a church or religious foundation.

ancient times in a clearing in woodland. By the nineteenth century the green, where fairs and sporting competitions were held, was often all that remained of the common land over which the cottagers had rights — to graze, and collect firewood and acorns.

There were villages that owed their origin to a castle. Dwellings were provided for the small army of workmen needed to build and repair these great edifices, and in troublous times the people had felt protected from roving bands of robbers and lawless barons. Then, too, there were villages that had grown up around a church or religious foundation, which needed, as well as masons and carpenters, ploughmen to farm their land. Cottages, clustering 'like children holding the gown of their good mother', were built for the workers and a guest-house for pilgrims, which continued in existence as the village inn of later times.

A typical village with 'a neat or handsome parsonage and grey church set in the midst' was described in the nineteenth century by the novelist George Eliot:

> there was the pleasant tinkle of the blacksmith's anvil, the
> patient carthorses waiting at his door; the basket-maker
> peeling his willow wands in the sunshine; the wheelwright
> putting the last touch to a blue cart with red wheels; here
> and there a cottage with bright transparent windows
> showing pots full of blooming balsams or geraniums, and
> little gardens in front all double daisies or dark wallflowers;
> at the well, clean comely women carrying yoked buckets,
> and towards the free school small Britons dawdling on, and
> handling their marbles in the pockets of unpatched
> corduroys adorned with brass buttons.

Left: Cottages perched on rocks beside a river in Lyndale, Devon.

Left: From the village and from cottages in the surrounding countryside people gather to watch a Punch and Judy show.

Above: The brick-paved Walks at Groombridge in Kent with its neat row of eighteenth-century tile-hung cottages. Groombridge was an estate village.

In Hampshire is the village made famous in the previous century by the naturalist Gilbert White. Selborne consisted of a single straggling street, or cartway, where the square piece of open ground surrounded by cottages was known as 'The Plestor'. Until it was ravaged in a great storm a vast oak stood in the middle of the green, with a short squat body, and huge horizontal arms extending almost to the extremity of the area. This venerable tree, with stone steps around the trunk, and seats above them, 'was the delight of old and young, and a place of much resort in summer evenings; where the former sat in grave debate, while the latter frolicked and danced before them.'

With the hamlet of Oakhanger, and counting those living in the single farms and scattered dwellings on the edge of the forest, there were upwards of 670 inhabitants. 'We abound with poor; many of whom are sober and industrious, and live comfortably in good stone or brick cottages, which are glazed, and have chambers above stairs: mud buildings we have none.'

Musing on a summer evening's walk through his parish, he wrote the lines:

> Each rural sight, each sound, each smell, combine;
> The tinkling sheep-bell, or the breath of kine;
> The new-mown hay that scents the swelling breeze,
> Or cottage-chimney smoking through the trees.

Also in the south of England, John Ruskin recalled from his childhood in the 1820s travelling a short distance in the neighbourhood of Shirley, in Kent. The road lay through a secluded district of field and wood:

> traversed here and there by winding lanes, and by one or
> two smooth mail-coach roads, beside which, at intervals of
> a mile or two, stood some gentleman's house, with its lawn,
> gardens, offices, and attached fields, indicating a country
> life of long continuance and quiet respectability. Except

Above: At West Tarring in Sussex, a fine Tudor dwelling. The oldest surviving buildings are often in village streets, rather than standing in isolation. The roof is of fine Horsham stone slabs.

Left: A village street in Kent. The small weather-boarded buildings in the middle of the row were probably workshops or built for storage.

such an one here and there, one saw no dwellings above the size of cottages or small farmsteads; these, wood-built usually, and thatched, their porches embroidered with honeysuckle, and their gardens with daisies, their doors mostly ajar, or with one half shut to keep in the children, and a bricked or tiled footway from it to the wicket gate, — all neatly kept, and vivid with a sense of the quiet energies of their contented tenants, — made the lane-turnings cheerful, and gleamed in half hidden clusters beneath the slopes of the wood-lands at Sydenham and Penge.

He remembered 'no signs of distress, of effort, or of change; many of enjoyment, and not a few of wealth beyond the daily needs of life.'

William Cobbett, on a tour of inspection in the north of England in 1832, found to his satisfaction that in North Shields, 'The working people seem to be very well off; their dwellings solid and clean, and their furniture good.' He described the countryside and remarked on some of the differences between this part of England and elsewhere:

These sides of the Tyne are very fine: corn-fields, woods, pastures, villages; a church every four miles, or thereabouts; cows and sheep beautiful; oak trees, though none very large; and, in short, a fertile and beautiful country, wanting only the gardens and the vine-covered cottages that so beautify the counties in the South and the West. All the buildings are of stone. Here are coal-works and railways every now and then . . . but the little gardens and orchards are wanting.

Left: The harsh reality of winter in the countryside: a mother and six young children chop and collect wood for the cottage fire.

Left: A farm boy leading
the carthorses along a
track beside a typical
Surrey cottage at
Chobham.

Above: A whitewashed
cottage at the edge of
the sea at Runswick Bay,
Yorkshire. The cottage
behind is derelict.

Left: A row of thatched cottages at Toller in Dorset. This would have housed at least three families.

Below: A single-storey cottage under a deep thatch in a secluded position in the countryside near Quidhampton, in the Nadder Valley near Salisbury.

In 1874 the Rev. Francis Kilvert revisited Clyro in Radnorshire, where he had been curate for seven years. He was known and loved by all in the parish, and as he came near the playground a ringing cheer went up from the children. His diary is a wonderful record of country life and country places in mid-Victorian times, and to him 'every foot of Clyro ground is classical and sacred and has its story':

> I love to wander on these soft gentle mournful autumn days, alone among the quiet peaceful solitary meadows, tracing out the ancient footpaths and mossy overgrown stiles between farm and hamlet, village and town, musing of the many feet that have trodden these ancient and now well nigh deserted and almost forgotten ways and walking in the footsteps of the generations that have gone before and passed away.

On 31 August 1874 he recorded sentimentally that he had set out:

Left: An old Surrey cottage of the type most admired by Helen Allingham, with a fine old brick chimney and lichen-covered tiling.

Below: A half-timbered cottage at Sandhills near Witley in Surrey. Helen Allingham moved from London to live here in 1881.

by the old familiar fields and the Beacon stile, and when I looked down upon the dear old village nestling round the Church in the hollow at the dingle mouth and saw the fringes of the beautiful woods and the hanging orchards and the green slopes of Penllan and the white farms and cottages dotted over the hills a thousand sweet and sad memories came over me and all my heart rose up within me and went out in love towards the beloved place and people among whom I lived so long and happily.

At that time Kilvert was curate to his father at Langley Burrell in Wiltshire, not far from Coate, the village where the writer and naturalist Richard Jefferies lived. Beyond the water-bailiff's cottage in Coate the buildings came in little groups:

some up crooked lanes, hidden away by elms as if out of sight in a cupboard, and some dotted along the brooks, scattered so that, unless you had connected them all with a very long rope, no stranger could have told which belonged to the village and which did not. They drifted into various tithings, and yet it was all the same place.

It was hard to say where the village ended and where the cottages became truly isolated, where no distant sounds of everyday life — the voices of children, the bark of a dog, the 'clangour' of geese, the chopping of wood — were to be heard on the breeze, and no sight

or smell of wood-smoke. It was often only on market days that the occasional passer-by was to be seen.

Snuggled into the side of a hill or in some sheltered place, carving a place for themselves in a brief clearing in the woods, these outlying cottages were the homes of labourers and woodmen and keepers. Jefferies's gamekeeper lived:

> in a sheltered combe, or narrow hollow of the woodlands, overshadowed by a mighty Spanish chestnut . . . The elms in the meadow are full of rooks' nests, and in the spring the coombe will resound with their cawing: these black bandits, who do not touch it at other times, will then ravage the garden to feed their hungry young, despite ingenious scarecrows.

Another cottage remembered by Jefferies had grown to its owner: 'The low thatched roof that had rounded itself and stooped down to fit itself to Job's shoulders.'

The cottagers' companions in these lonely places were the wild animals — the foxes and rabbits, the owls and squirrels, and the rooks — and scarce were the meetings with mortals outside the family circle.

Left: The ancient cross on the village green at Long Wittenham in Berkshire. It was probably put up by monks from the nearby priory. The cottages have dormer windows peeping through the thatch.

Left: A cottage on an ancient site by a ford, with sheep crossing over.

Right: The Post Office in Witley. Communication in rural Britain was far easier after the introduction of the penny post in Queen Victoria's reign.

CHAPTER II
The History of the Cottage

To give a cottage a precise date is an impossible task for who knows what lies beneath the accretions of centuries — the improved chimney, the layer of plaster for weatherproofing, the enlarged windows, the bargeboard or decorative porch added later. Many cottages too were almost certainly built using existing materials. A sturdy oak beam originally hewn in the Middle Ages, and growing harder and stronger with age, was a valuable asset and might well have been incorporated into an eighteenth-century cottage. Good blocks of stone — so hard and time-consuming to cut — might well have been appropriated from an abandoned castle or monastery nearby.

The exact date at which the 'hut' of the medieval peasant could be described as a 'cottage' is a moot point. The historian Dorothy Hartley, in *Life and Work of the People of England*, described the medieval landscape from her observations of illuminated manuscripts:

> There were deep dark forests, full of wild beasts, boars and
> wolves . . . there were marshy tracts dangerous to those who
> did not know the paths . . . No trim hedges separated the
> fields; the arable land in the average manor was divided, by
> ridges of earth, into three fields; two were sown with crops
> each year, while the third was left fallow, ready for next
> year's sowing. In this arable land every villager had his own
> little portions; each man had strips in different fields so that
> all might share fairly the better and the poorer soil. A great
> tract of grassland was by feudal custom 'common' to the use

Left: A cottage beneath the walls of the ruins of Thirlwall Castle in Northumberland. The water from the river would have been equally useful to both castle and cottage.

Left: A poor fisherman and his family in their cottage by the sea. Fishing tackle hangs by the door to dry and a spinning wheel stands in the corner of the room.

Right: The massive roughly-hewn beam extends over the hearth. The crockery on the dresser and the mantel shelf would have been the cottager's most prized possessions.

of everyone for the pasturing of cattle; swine were herded in the great oakwoods that bordered the manor lands . . . The villeins lived in little thatched huts of wood or earth, consisting as a rule of one single room, with a hole for a chimney, windows with wooden shutters, and rough and scanty furniture.

So flimsy were these dwellings that it was common during this period for villeins absconding from their manors simply to knock down their houses and carry the

The cruck form of
this cottage
represents an early
and simple form of
cottage building.

Cottages near Bearstead, Kent. Wooden frames for drying hay are to be seen in the field opposite the cottages.

materials with them to start afresh elsewhere. At the same time, a villein, behind with his dues to the manor, might be punished by having his hut demolished. Storms were known to have blown down entire villages of such dwellings. 'I'll huff and I'll puff and I'll blow your house down', as the old nursery rhyme goes. The term 'house breaking' dates from this period, and refers to thieves literally 'breaking' the house in order to rob it. Clearly from the time of the Conquest up to the fourteenth or fifteenth century the home of the average peasant was a fairly pitiful affair: the poet William Langland, who wrote the earliest poetry in the English vernacular, used the anglo-saxon words 'povere mennes cotes' to describe a cottage in his most important work, *Piers Plowman.*

In the early medieval period 'cottages' certainly did not last for longer than a generation, and needed constant rebuilding. They would have been constructed of whatever was available: timber, turf, mud and thatching materials such as heather or fern, all of which could have been collected, as of right, from the common land. Any tools used would have been fairly primitive. One room would have housed the whole family and, probably, the odd animal. The floor would have been beaten earth.

The earliest cottages to survive from the medieval period are called 'cruck' cottages, the name describing a particular type of construction where the main beams are curved or bent. Different dialects all over the country gave these great beams other names: 'crooks', 'crucks', 'siles', 'levers', or in Yorkshire 'a pair of forks'. Cruck cottages were an advance on the hut, as their very survival demonstrates. Vast forests of oak trees covered much of Britain, and these structures show how the

cottage builder was from the start extraordinarily inventive in searching out materials from his immediate vicinity and using them to the best possible purpose.

The cruck beams were erected in two pairs, like a couple of wishbones, and held fast by a ridge beam (across the ridge of the roof) and tie beams (making the wishbone into an 'A'). Since the pairs of cruck beams were usually split from the same piece of timber, we can assume that the skill of a carpenter or 'wright', as he was then called, was needed. He would have selected the timber from the standing trees, searching out those with great curving branches with the right angle and length. The carpenter would have split it into usable sections and pegged the structure together while it lay on the ground. Raising up the edifice with ropes must have been a communal effort, no doubt accompanied by some form of celebration.

At first the cottages had no foundations, and the base of each beam was charred to prevent it rotting in the ground; later developments led to the beams being dropped into a rough stone base, and subsequently the building of a foundation wall. The problem with this structure was the lack of an upright wall. This was solved by extending the tie-beam and allowing it to project at either end. A vertical wall could thus be created with beams placed from the foot of the building.

Once the basic timber structure was erected, the less skilled work of creating wall panels with wattle and daub was presumably done by the inhabitant. Wattle is a panel of wooden rods, sufficiently bendy to interweave; this was usually made from hazel, but examples of elm, maple, aspen and birch have been found. If the rods were too thick they were split. The whole wattle was covered with 'daub', or clay, which was often mixed with straw, cow-dung or chalk: whatever was locally available and known to make an easily workable mixture.

That wattle and daub was such a widespread technique throughout Britain is reflected in the range of dialect words for it, such as 'stake and rice' (Scotland), 'stud and mud' (Lincolnshire), 'daub and stower' (Yorkshire) and 'rad and dab' (Cheshire and Lancashire). Holes were left in the roof — probably protected from

Right: Throughout the history of cottages people have lived in close proximity to their animals; this barn would have been attached to the cottage.

the weather by some form of louvre — for the smoke from the fire, which was lit on the floor in the centre of the hut. The purpose of the smoke hole and the window were the same: to provide ventilation, rather than light. Early words for window suggest this purpose: 'wind eye' and 'wind-dur' (wind door), and many were probably no more than slits. It is thought that the very early window probably had a shutter in the form of a piece of wood that hung from the top. This could be propped open with a stick, rather in the manner of an awning.

The whole cottage would have been thatched. A rich diversity of styles, methods and materials were used in thatching. Since thatch needs to be replaced regularly, this is one of the most ephemeral of crafts and we cannot surmise precisely how medieval thatch looked. This was the basic building form which could either be extended lengthways by adding extra pairs of cruck beams. Each section was called a 'bay' and amounted to about sixteen feet. This term was sometimes used to describe a measurement: a bay of hay or grain. Another way of enlarging the cottage was to create a lean-to at one end.

Such is the nature of man that the history of cottage building is a long search for greater convenience and comfort. The cruck cottage had its limitations: not only were the great curved pieces of wood hard to find in some areas, but also the beams curved inconveniently, taking up valuable space in an already cramped area. And it was not easy to create the upper floor that must have struck many inhabitants as desirable: a place off the damp floor — and maybe away from all manner of wildlife — which would be good as sleeping quarters and for storage. These improvements came with the Tudor age, when a new and far more flexible method of building came into use: the timber-framed cottage as we see it today,

the technical term for which is 'post and truss'.

Chaucer has left us with a description in *The Canterbury Tales* of the widow's cottage in the 'Nun's Priest's Tale':

A poure widewe somdel stoupen in age,
Was whilom dwelling in a narwe cotage,
Beside a grove, stonding in a dale.
This widewe, which I tell you of my tale,
Sin thilke day that she was last a wif,
In patience led a ful simple lif.
For litel was hire catel and hire rente:
By husbondry of swiche as God hire sente,
She found hireself, and eke hire doughtren two.
Three large sowes had she, and no mo
Three kine and eke a sheep that highte Malle.
Ful sooty was hire boure, and eke hire halle,
In which she ete many a slender mele.
Of poinant sauce ne knew she never a dele.
No deintee morsel passed thurgh hire throte:
Hire diete was accordant to hire cote . . .
A yerd she had, enclosed all about
With stickes, and a drie diche without,
In which she had a cok highte Chaunteclere
In all the land of crowing n'as his pere.

Geoffrey Chaucer's birth date is unknown, but it is presumed to be about 1340. The 1340s were marked by one of the worst episodes of the plague in Britain, the 'Black Death' or the 'Great Pestilence', as it was known. Roughly carved in Latin on the church tower of the village of Ashwell in Hertfordshire is the legend '1350, wretched, wild, distracted. The dregs of the people alone survive to tell the tale.' It

Left: An old cottage in the Sussex village of Bignor, dating from Tudor times. Built in three bays, the two outer bays have a jettied upper storey. This was the dwelling of a yeoman.

is thought that up to one in three of the population perished during the second half of that century with the result that, as families died off, land became available and labour was scarce. The old manorial system and its authority declined, and it became possible for villeins to move to find better land and maybe a kinder and more generous landlord. In place of the old feudal system a system of leasing land for rent came into being, and a new class of person, the smallholder, emerged.

Due to the shortage of manpower, a labour market developed for the rural workforce and the labourer had money — very little, but some. At the same time skills developed as separate crafts: men specialized as masons, thatchers, tilers, carpenters. They built for the 'cottage industries': for the wool worker, the tanner and the weaver.

A new breed of energetic yeoman, or tenant farmer, was also emerging, with his own responsibilities and ideas about farming the land. Farming too became more specialized, and sheep farming a more profitable alternative to labour-intensive crop raising. This involved creating pastureland for the sheep, and in some places landlords would clear old villages and field systems to create it: the first of the 'enclosures'. These shifts in social patterns and changes in ways of life led to what many have termed the golden age of cottage building, coinciding with the dawn of the Tudor Age

The reign of Queen Elizabeth I has long captured the imagination of the British people: as Stewart Dick wrote in *The Cottage Homes of England*, which was published in 1909:

> From a dim twilight we suddenly seem to step into bright sunshine. In every department of life there is an astonishing outburst of vigour. The fruits which have been slowly ripening for centuries seem suddenly to come to maturity. England is awake after the slumbers of the Middle Ages, and for a brief period the national life blazes with unprecedented brilliance and splendour.

As one writer said, 'There is nothing obtrusive about the old cottages. They do not dominate the landscape, but are content to be part of it, and to pass unnoticed unless one looks specially for their homely beauties.'

The poet Robert Herrick, who was born towards the end of Queen Elizabeth's reign, wrote a poem, *The Country Life,* which gives an idyllic picture of English life:

> For sports, for pageantry, and plays,
> Thou has thy eves and holidays,
> On which the young men and maid meet
> To exercise their dancing feet,
> Tripping the comely country round,
> With daffodils and daisies crowned.
> Thy wakes, thy quintals, here thou hast,
> Thy Maypoles too with garlands graced;
> Thy morris-dance, thy Whitsun-ale,
> Thy shearing-feast, which never fail;
> Thy harvest home, thy wassail bowl,
> That's tossed up after fox th' hole;
> Thy mummeries, thy Twelfthtide kings
> And queens, thy Christmas revellings;
> Thy nut-brown mirth, thy russet wit,
> And no man pays too dear for it.

William Harrison, rector of Radwinter in Essex, observed in 1577:

> Never so much oke hath been spent in a hundred years before as in ten years of our time, for everie man almost is a builder, and he that hath bought any small parcel of ground, be it ever so little, will not be quiet till he have pulled downe the old house, if anie were there standing, and set up a new after his own device.

A jettied upper storey, a typical feature of medieval cottages.

The doorway of a cottage near Witley in Surrey. The ledge at the bottom of the door would have served to hold the planks together and protect the wood at the bottom from rotting.

A honeysuckle-draped porch with the vestiges of paintwork on the well-worn door.

Of early cottages he wrote:

> In times past men were contented to dwell in houses builded of sallow, willow, plum-tree, hardbeane, and elme, so that the use of oke was in maner dedicated whole unto churches, religious houses, princes' palaces, noblemen's lodgings, and navigation, but now all these are rejected, and nothing but oke anie whit regarded. In those days the courage of the owner was a sufficient defence to keepe the house in safetie, but now the assurance of the timber double doores, lockes, and bolts, must defend the man from robbing.

Such was the need and passion for building during this period that it is likely that many cottages were conversions of old farm buildings, rather as today cottages are created by converting Victorian schoolhouses, coach houses, even redundant 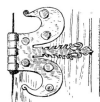 barns, windmills and churches. One of the most picturesque rows of cottages in England, Arlington Row in Bibury, Gloucestershire, started its life as a late fourteenth-century monastic sheephouse. Then, as now, there were planning acts. In 1589 an act was passed (though impossible to enforce) which stated that no cottage might be built on a plot of land smaller than four acres, and that if it was, it could be pulled down forthwith. This was intended to prevent people appropriating areas of common land as their own, a practice known as 'encroachment'.

It was from the apparently inexhaustible supply of oak that the new cottages were built. Post and truss buildings may vary vastly in the finished effect and size, and clearly none look as they did when they were built, but the method was straightforward. A low foundation of brick or stone was made and onto this were placed horizontal beams; upright posts were then fixed onto these.

Although many of the cottages would have been built as single-storey dwellings,

Left: A visitor to a Scottish cottage, with the family grouped around the most basic type of hearth.

Right: Mullion windows with leaded panes on this stone cottage.

using this type of construction it became relatively simple to create an upper storey, which during this early period was frequently cantilevered out. This was called a 'jetty', or 'jutty'. The reasons for this fashion are not quite clear, although a plausible suggestion is that it provided more stability for the upper floor. An advantage was that it gave some protection from the weather to the lower storey, acting almost like a porch. The upper floor was made of timber joists with boards of wood laid across them, usually oak, and between the beams (roughly cut and some with their bark still on) there would be an infilling of clay, chopped straw or interlaced hazel sticks. The rough finish would, of course, have been visible from the room below, and as people's sensibilities increased they began to plaster it over, creating the beamed ceiling that is such a familiar and integral part of the old timber-frame country cottage.

During this period window openings were more like something that we would recognize today, although they certainly remained very small in size. Glass was a

Left: A fine central chimney on a cottage at Elmley Castle in Worcestershire. The moulded top is finely crafted in brick.

luxury, and out of the question for the cottager, who would keep the weather out with oiled canvas stretched across the hole, or a latticework of wattle. It was discovered that diamond-shaped lattice was more effective than squared, and when glazing did eventually become commonplace the diamond pane was for many years the norm.

All evidence points to entrances being the main source of light within a cottage — paintings as late as the nineteenth century showing the door wide open in all but the most inclement weather. It is probable that the 'door' to the early hut was no more than a skin, bundles of furze or interwoven straw. The earliest proper doors would have been what are termed 'batten' doors, the upright boards being fixed together with a horizontal batten or ledge, and in many areas these were traditionally bisected in the manner of a stable door. An old term for this is a 'heck' door. It is easy to see how convenient this would have been for keeping children, animals and weather in — or out. The earliest way of securing the door would have been from the inside, with a wooden bar that crossed the door and fitted into slots on the wall on either side. This cumbersome method would have been superseded by the latch, which had the advantage of working from inside and out.

One of the most welcome and effective improvements in cottage building was made by placing the hearth at the gable end of the building, rather than in the centre of the main room. This would not have become commonplace until the second half of the sixteenth century. However, smoking chimneys must always have remained a problem, as is shown in this description of the interior of an Elizabethan cottage from a contemporary poem:

> Of one bay's breadth, God wot! a silly cote,
> Whose thatched spars are furr'd with sluttish soote
> A whole inch thick, shining like black-moor's brows,
> Through smok that down the headless barrell blows . . .

The open fire was a constant hazard, with all the attendant dangers of a spark setting

off the whole edifice. The building of a chimney must have improved the safety of the fire and vastly reduced the amount of smoke in the cottage. The warmed chimney bricks would have also provided a modicum of heat to the floor above.

The creation of chimneys goes hand-in-hand with the development of brick-making in Britain, since they could only really be built satisfactorily with brick or stone, early attempts having been made using lathe and plaster or wattle and clay. In the early days brick was an imported luxury from the Low Countries, but once home-grown brick-making became established they became an economic possibility. These chimney can often be seen built onto the ends of cottages, their width at the base reflecting the size of the inglenook hearth within. At the same time a small bake oven, leading off the main chimney, was sometimes added.

The fact that the cottages were becoming more pleasant places in which to live, and pride of ownership, is reflected in the little flourishes of ornament that begin to appear during the sixteenth century. Scrolls of foliage and curious animals might be carved along a beam or post, delicate mouldings on window frames; plasterwork provided a smooth surface on which patterns could be pricked, incised or moulded. Even the humble mud floor might be improved, in the method described by Sir Hugh Platt in his book *The Jewel House of Art and Nature*. Written in 1594, he recommended that mixing ox blood with the clay would provide a smooth, glistening and hard floor. There is also evidence that small animal bones were driven into the floor, not only patterning it but also making it more hard-wearing.

The seventeenth century was a period of greater upheaval than the previous one, spanning the Civil War, religious interference and the Glorious Revolution. In terms of cottage building it was probably one of slow improvement, as the newer and more advanced building techniques filtered down the scale. There would have been a more confident use of building materials such as brick and stone, resulting in better chimneys and the occasional use of tiles and stone tiles for roofing — far more long-lasting than thatch. In stone-quarrying areas stone-flagged floors would have appeared. Windows became more efficient, and the use of dormer windows

Left: The bread oven is clearly visible in its position to one side of the hearth.

would have made upper floors far more comfortable. Glass became less of a luxury and must have appeared in a few of the cottages of the more well to-do. To begin with the glass was fixed, providing what must have seemed a miraculous draught-free view, but gradually the opening casement window was adopted. Cottages also increased in dimensions, and there were variations from the basic medieval one-room plan.

The logic of building a chimney in the centre of the cottage, where it would heat far more of the building, rather than at the end wall, became apparent, and gradually became standard practice. This tended to lead to a cottage having two downstairs rooms. The space beside the chimney breast was sometimes used to build a narrow winding stair to the upper floor, and this can often be seen in paintings of old cottage interiors. This replaced the simpler solution of placing a ladder straight up through a hole in the upper floor. A straight enclosed staircase would not have been built in a cottage prior to the seventeeth century.

The survival of the cottages built up until this period depended on a wide variety of economic and social factors. One important consideration would have been whether the village was a so-called 'closed' village, owned by one family, and therefore closed to outside influences, or an 'open' village, where the land was owned by both landlords and independent freeholders, and there was far more freedom to expand. Open villages were far more sprawling in character, with a much wider variety of cottages; some maybe very small, built by families squatting or encroaching on common land, and some more substantial, belonging to rural craftsmen. The inhabitants of closed villages tended to be inhabited only by agricultural labourers.

In the eighteenth century the lives of the cottagers, and the landscape in which they lived, was affected by the second great wave of enclosures, causing the virtual disappearance of the old open-field farming system. The number of wealthy landowners had vastly increased (as smallholders had declined), and great strides forward were being made in farming techniques. Land became far more profitable, so landowners, naturally, wanted more control over it to practise these

Left: The hipped gable end and weather-boarding make this cottage typical of the south-eastern counties. The long 'catslide' roof at the back was a common way of extending cottages.

Left: These single-storey squatters' cottages on the side of a muddy lane show how insubstantial many dwellings still were in the nineteenth century.

Below: Selworthy in Somerset, one of the cottages built as part of a picturesque scheme in the Regency period.

new high-yielding methods. The old village fields and common lands were enclosed by hedges and fences, and the whole concept of private land was extended. During this process cottages, and in many cases whole villages, were swept away, causing great hardship. The writer William Cobbett recalled a village before enclosure:

> I used to go around a little common, called Horton Heath, on a Sunday. I found the husbands at home. The common contained about 150 acres; and I found round the skirts of it, and near to the skirts, about thirty cottages and gardens, the latter chiefly encroachments on the common, which was waste (as it was called) . . . I remember one hundred and twenty-five or thirty-five stall of bees, worth at that time ten shillings a stall, at least. Cows there were about fifteen, besides heifers and calves; about sixty pigs great and small; and not less than five hundred heads of poultry.

He then stated emphatically:

> I learn'd to hate a system that could lead English gentlemen to disregard matters like these! That could induce them to tear up 'wastes' and sweep away occupiers like those I have described! . . . Was it a 'waste' when a hundred, perhaps of healthy boys and girls were playing there of a Sunday, instead of creeping about covered with filth in the alleys of a town.

There was another threat to the existence of the cottage communities: the landowner, often newly enriched — and maybe ennobled — set about creating the perfect backdrop for his house. This was the great period of country-house building, and few landowners did not aspire to an elegant Palladian mansion set

in an exquisite landscape park dotted with lakes and clumps of trees, and maybe even a little classical temple for picnics on a fine summer's day. If a cottage or village stood inconveniently close to the house, or appeared as a blot on the view, it was a small matter to demolish it. This was the subject of Oliver Goldsmith's famous poem *The Deserted Village,* in which he described the imaginary village of Auburn as it had been:

> How often have I paused on every charm,
> The sheltered cot, the cultivated farm,
> The never failing brook, the busy mill,
> The decent church that topt the neighbouring hill,
> The hawthorn bush, with seats beneath the shade,
> For talking age and whispering lovers made.

And as it had become:

> But times are altered; trade's unfeeling train
> Usurp the land and dispossess the swain;
> Along the lawn, where scattered hamlets rose,
> Unwieldy wealth, and cumbrous pomp repose;
> And every want to opulence allied,
> And every pang that folly pays to pride.

Of course the eighteenth-century landowner still needed to house his labourers, and on many estates new cottages were built in neat rows outside the gates of the park. These were often designed by the architect of the great house, or chosen from a pattern book, a catalogue of designs, such as *A Series of Plans for Cottages or Habitations of the Labourer,* published by John Wood in 1781. These cottages were undoubtedly a vast improvement on the earlier habitations, and many landowners took pride in improving not only their land but also the conditions of

Left: Cowdray's Cottage at Midhurst in Sussex: an old building with picturesque additions in the form of a rustic porch and verandah.   65

their employees. Wood himself had noted that existing cottages were often 'dirty, inconvenient, miserable hovels', and that 'It is melancholy to see a man and his wife, and sometimes half a dozen children crowded together in the same room,

nay often in the same bed . . .' His plans dictated that the cottage should be built on brick or stone foundations, and that the rooms should be no less than eight feet high and facing south or east. They did not have to be 'fine,' he wrote, 'yet I recommend regularity, which is beauty; regularity will render them ornaments to the country, instead of their being as at present disagreeable objects.' It was also considered helpful to build cottages in pairs, ensuring that the main entrances were at the side 'in order to avoid the appearance of any uncleanly habits', as one author put it.

At the beginning of the nineteenth century fashion dictated a change: regularity was no longer admired as a model of all that was fine and beautiful and, instead, an enthusiasm for the 'picturesque' held sway. For the Regency landowner the cottage was perceived as an 'ornament', a little thatched place dropped prettily into the landscape. If the cottage already existed, it might be improved with decoration considered appropriate for a rural labourer: a trellised porch for instance, with creeper intertwined, under whose shade the labourer might rest 'after the fatigues of the day', or perhaps the addition of bargeboards carved with curls and curves.

During the period there was in fact a shortage of rural housing, and much of what existed was in a state of decay and dereliction. Many landowners therefore built anew, and some even built whole villages of picturesque cottages. Books were published containing black-and-white and colour plates illustrating plans and elevations for the perfect picturesque cottage. Assymetry was essential, thatch, elaborately leaded windows (hexagonal and lozenge-shaped panes were much admired), porches, overhanging eaves, elaborate chimneys and plantings of

'After Four Centuries', as Helen Allingham entitled this watercolour, with reference to the unchanged charm. 'All the little eccentricities of form which give character, and endear those cottages to us, are faithfully delineated.'

climbers and creepers were all important elements.

The earliest picturesque village was Blaise Hamlet, built near Bristol in the early nineteenth century. A contemporary description of the ten cottages grouped round a green reads:

> The air of comfort diffused over these little dwellings, the play of light and shadow produced by their projections and recesses, which afford shelter to a variety of creeper, the highly ornamental and varied character of the chimnies; and the beauty of the surrounding little gardens, glittering throughout the summer with flowers of brightest hues, and guarded from the intruding hand by hedges of sweet-briar, suggest the most pleasing images to the fancy, and shed a romantic and poetical character over this favoured asylum.

Blaise was built for the elderly employees of a Quaker called John Harford, but the fashion for the so-called *cottage ornée* spread beyond the mere labourer's cottage into the realm of middle-class family housing.

It is interesting that one description of the Blaise cottages, written nearly twenty years after they were built, reads: 'a visit to them has long formed a favourite excursion from the village of Clifton and the city of Bristol', and it was noted that they offered 'a variety of subjects for the pencil'. The paintings and watercolours of the artists in this book were also searching for the picturesque.

Stewart Dick, whose text accompanies the watercolours of Helen Allingham, expressed admiration that 'Every twist of the old oak beams is shown, every curve in the roof, for it has sunk down on the rafter, so that the rows of tiles undulate like ripples on a sandy shore . . . All the little eccentricities of form which give character, and endear those cottages to us, are faithfully delineated.' It is recognition that the small cottage is a crucial, though unobtrusive, factor in the beauty of the British landscape.

A cottage in the
Lake District, an
area where there
was no alternative
building material
to stone. Later
owners might well
have given this
cottage a roof of
the characteristic
greenish slate, as
lasting longer
than thatch.

CHAPTER III

Traditions in Cottage Building

We all know the rich variety that there is in the landscape of Britain: wooded valleys, rolling hills, heath, forest, breck, moor, chalk downs, flat fens, highlands and uplands, coastal cliffs and limestone escarpments. All these differences are apparent in the cottages, and sometimes, within a matter of a few miles, they will change from stone to brick, from cob to half-timbered. Not only does the basic building material change but also the outer shell. The constant fight to keep cottages warm and dry in the face of the elements has led to their having a variety of protective coverings — and these too vary from region to region: tile-hanging in Surrey and Sussex, plaster and pargetting in East Anglia, timber weather-boarding in Kent and Essex, slate-hanging in Wales and Cornwall and harling in Scotland.

The most basic building material is cob. This is essentially mud mixed with whatever is available locally: straw, heather, grit, sand, gravel, chalk or fragments of slate, known as 'shilf'. Cob cottages are most commonly found in the south-west of England, although they were built all over the British Isles where the earth was suitable. There is a Devonshire saying that all cob wants is a good pair of shoes (a stone foundation) and a good hat (a well-thatched roof), and then it will last forever.

Above: A cob cottage at Paignton in south Devon, the thickness of the wall clearly visible in the deep window openings and massive chimney.

Left: A primitive stone single-storey cottage in the Welsh hills. The thatch was in all likelihood made of heather, and the stone would have been collected from the land around.

The process of building was slow and not particularly skilled, with the walls being alternately built up and left to dry until the entire wall was a sun-baked whole. The novelist and poet Thomas Hardy described cob-building in his native Dorset:

> What was called mud-wall was really a composition of chalk, clay and straw . . . This was mixed up into a sort of dough-pudding close to where the cottage was to be built. The mixing was performed by treading and shovelling — women sometimes being called in to tread, and the straw was added to bind the mass together . . . It was then thrown by pitchforks on to the wall, where it was trodden down to a thickness of about two feet, till a rise of about three feet had been reached. This was left to settle for a day or two . . .

As the walls grew higher, the layers became shallower: they were usually about three feet deep, characteristically with curved corners, since a sharp edge was hard to make and more likely to crack. The enemy of cob was damp, which caused it to crumble and disintegrate, so the finished wall was given a good coating of plaster or roughcast and painted, the wall footing often being covered with pitch or tar. A deep thatched roof projected well over the walls. With regional differences came regional words: the yellowish earth walls of Buckinghamshire were made of 'wichert', while Cornish 'clob' cottages incorporated the shilf, in Pembrokeshire they were known as 'clom cottages' and those in Cumbria as 'clay daubins'.

The collector of folk tales and songs S. Baring-Gould wrote in 1898 that many of the old cob cottages were disappearing because of the heavy insurance rates on thatch. The roof timbers were not designed to hold the weight of slates or tiles, so that cottages were pulled down and rebuilt:

Left: A crofter's cottage in the Highlands of Scotland. Thatch on cottages in the Islands and Highlands was traditionally weighted down with a network of ropes and stones to prevent it blowing off. Turf was also sometimes used.

Then in place of a lovely old building with its windows under thatch, and the latter covering it soft and brown and warm as the skin of a mole, arises a piece of hideousness that is perhaps more commodious, but hardly so comfortable. I know that labourers who have been transferred from old cob cottages under thatch to new brick cottages under slate complain bitterly that they are losers in coziness by the exchange.

There is no greater contrast to the cob cottage than one built of stone. Stone cottages appear, naturally enough, wherever the stone was easily quarried, often areas where wood was, in any case, scarce. Stone is by far the most valuable building material and was chosen where possible for the most important buildings in the landscape: castles, churches, grand houses. It was rarely used for cottages until the seventeenth century, when the price of timber rose dramatically. Quarrying and cutting stone is highly skilled work. A remark by an old quarryman quoted in Alec Clifton Taylor's book *The Pattern of English Building* demonstrates this:

> Stone is a miracle of nature. No two quarries are alike and all stones vary within the same quarry. The correct selection taxes the skill of the quarryman. A quarry is like a book written in a strange language: it must be studied and understood.

For grand buildings a type of stone might have been used that had to be brought from afar, at considerable expense — St Paul's Cathedral in London was built of stone quarried at Taynton, near Burford in Oxfordshire — but for cottages the stone was unlikely to have come from more than a mile or two away.

British cottages were built of three main types of stone: limestone, sandstone and granite. Within those categories, and in addition to them, are others, whose

names are familiar: ragstone, millstone grit, chalk, puddingstone, slate, flint, ironstone, greenstone, and those named for where they came from, such as Ham Hill, Portland, Hornton and Purbeck.

In some stony areas, such as parts of Cumberland, the Yorkshire moors, Dartmoor, north Wales and the Scottish Highlands, primitive cottages were made from stones that were simply collected from the land around and built up into walls using precisely the same method as a dry-stone wall or a cairn. The boulders would have been broken up and shaped as far as the builder was able — no easy task with granite. The interstices would have been stuffed with earth and mud or smaller stones to improve the weatherproofing and draughtproofing, and then sometimes plastered over. These cottages were often of no more than one storey since it was difficult to incorporate the beams for an upper floor; the plan tended therefore to be extended lengthways on one floor.

They were often whitewashed, as can be learnt from the description of William Wordsworth's cottage written by his fellow poet Thomas de Quincey: '. . . a few green fields; and beyond them just two bowshots from the water a little white cottage gleaming in the midst of trees, with a vast and seemingly never-ending series of ascents.'

It is a white-painted gate that leads Jane Eyre to safety in her desperate nocturnal search on the Yorkshire moorland for shelter. Beyond she finds a cottage:

> black, low and rather long. In seeking the door, I turned an angle; there shot out the friendly gleam again, from the lozenged panes of a very small latticed window, within a foot of the ground, made still smaller by the growth of ivy or some

Above: A stone cottage on the Isle of Wight; thatch usually only lasted a generation before it needed replacing.

Left: Watermills, such as this one near Pitlochry in Perthshire, usually had a cottage attached. The stone gable incorporates a dovecot.

Left: A large circular stone chimney with cowl, characteristic of the village of Allerford in Somerset. It is likely that regional peculiarities such as this evolved over hundreds of years as the best solution to the problem of smoking chimneys.

Left: A timber-frame cottage near Cheltenham, only a few miles from the Cotswold stone one above at Whittington in Gloucestershire, illustrating the transition in building materials from one area to another.

other creeping plant, whose leaves clustered over the portion of the house in which it was set. The aperture was so screened and narrow, that curtain or shutter had been deemed unnecessary; and when I stooped down and put aside the spray of foliage shooting over it, I could see all within.

Charlotte Brontë knew these moorland cottages well from her life at Haworth in west Yorkshire, and in the same novel she described how Jane Eyre came to love the 'grey, small, antique structure, with its low roof, its latticed casements, its mouldering walls, its avenue of aged firs — all grown aslant under the stress of mountain winds; its garden dark with yew and holly — and where no flowers but of the hardiest species would bloom.'

In contrast to these cottages are the ones built in the Cotswolds, which in the sixteenth and seventeenth centuries was an area of great wealth. The sweeping upland had no trees for building but provided the pasture for sheep, whose wool was famed and prized throughout Britain and Europe. The prosperity that this brought to the towns and villages is reflected not only in the wonderful churches and merchants' and mill-owners' houses, but in the quality of cottage building. Almost every village had its own quarry of the creamy golden limestone. It was easy to work when newly quarried, then it hardened and turned greyer with time and exposure to the elements. Even quite simple cottages had carved mullions to the windows, dripstones up above them and characteristically steep gables, occasionally ornamented by a tablet chiselled with the date and initials of the first owner or builder.

Above: An old Sussex cottage with a typical roof of large sandstone slabs. It is possible to see that the roof timbers have sagged under the weight of the stone.

Left: Dove Cottage, Grasmere, the lakeland home of William and Dorothy Wordsworth. Dorothy describes how she papered the wall of one bedroom with old newspaper for extra warmth.

Cotswold cottages were roofed with the same stone as the walls. The old method of making the roofing-slates was to cut the stone slabs during the summer months and then leave them out of doors all winter. They would be kept wet so that frost caused the stone to develop fissures, leaving them very easy to split into manageable-sized slates. They would then have a hole cut in the top and be hung onto the rafters with wooden pegs, the thinnest slates being placed at the top of the roof and the thickest by the eaves.

Cotswold stone tiles were heavy (every hundred square foot weighs nearly a ton), and they therefore required strong roof timbers; but it was reckoned that, if properly made, they would last for hundreds of years. Stone gradually replaced thatch roofing in many other areas of Britain besides the Cotswolds: in Northamptonshire, Derbyshire, Yorkshire, along the Welsh border and in Surrey and Sussex, where the famous Horsham stone was widely used. These tiles were of sandstone, bigger and clumsier than the Cotswold limestone slates and consequently used on a less steeply pitched roof. Their colour tended to be darker.

The third category of stone roof was slate, which was quarried in the Lake District, Cornwall and Devon, north Wales and Leicestershire. The advantage of slate was that it was very hard and resistant to frost; it also split into thin tiles and was therefore comparatively light and easy to support. Its use grew vastly in the eighteenth and nineteenth centuries, when improved transport made it economically viable to quarry slate in Wales and transport it all over the British Isles. The dark grey Welsh slate could be made into the thinnest, smoothest tiles. The silvery-grey Cornish slate, the brownish Devon slate and the green and blue Lake District slates were all used on local cottages. Apart from it use as a roofing material, long slabs of slate were used for doorsteps, porches and garden paths. Many cottages in south Devon, Cornwall, Wales and the Lake District also have their walls hung with slates to provide extra warmth and protection against the weather. This was particularly popular in seaside areas, where south-westerly gales made weatherproofing a priority.

Left: A cottage at Redlynch in Wiltshire demonstrating how an upper floor has been tucked in under the roof.

Top right: Braemore in Hampshire. It can be clearly seen how a two-storey brick extension has been added onto the single-storey timber-frame cottage.

Bottom right: The difference in the shades of brick used to infill between the timbers in this cottage near Church Stretton in Shropshire suggests that the work was only done as and when necessary, and at different times.

Cottages rarely have the smooth ashlar face of properly dressed stone, unless they were built by a landlord of substance who was determined to display a grand face to the outside world. They were more usually built of what is called 'rubblestone'. 'Rubble' is the name given to the small irregularly-shaped stone, of any type, easily collected from the land or from quarries, and used for walls. This method of building ideally needed plenty of mortar to hold the cottage together. The mortar was composed of coarse sand mixed with slaked lime and water, which set into an impermeable bond. Occasionally, tiny chips of flint were set into the mortar to strengthen it, a technique known as 'galleting'. Flints were also used for rubble masonry, particularly in seaside areas where the stones could be picked off the beach, such as Suffolk, Norfolk and Sussex. On grander buildings the flints were skilfully cut, or 'knapped', to expose the dark quartz centre of the flint, but with simple cottages it was much more usual to use the whole stone, in the manner of a cobble. These flints were often combined with courses of stone or brick. Stone that was considered unsuitable for larger buildings was sometimes used for cottages: pudding-stone (a material which consists of little pebbles and gravel naturally cemented together) in the Thames valley and chalk in Dorset and Wiltshire.

Cement came into use in the mid-nineteenth century. It was the hard uniform colour and texture of cement, combined with the machine-made mass-produced bricks of the period, that led to the appreciation of the brick cottages from earlier times. The bricks had often been made by itinerant brickmakers, and the wide range of subtle colourings derived from the differences in the clays and in the firing processes.

Hand-made bricks were time-consuming to make. The clay and the firing had to be exactly right to achieve relatively uniform uncracked bricks. Where there was plenty of stone, as in the Cotswolds or the Pennines, bricks were rarely used, but in other areas, such as East Anglia and Berkshire, the convenience and long-lasting qualities of brick were soon appreciated. Landowners building cottages at the end of the eighteenth and into the nineteenth century would certainly have considered

Above: In the Devil's Punchbowl under Hindhead in Surrey a cottage has 'weather-tiling' covering the top storey.

Left: Old clay tiles on a jumble of roofs of some weather-boarded cottages in Godalming, Surrey.

An old cottage at Hagbourne in Berkshire with a plastered finish. The windows have stone or painted wood ledges over them to help prevent the wooden casements from rotting.

a brick cottage a good investment, and when the architect John Wood published *A Series of Plans for Cottages or Habitations of the Labourer* in 1781 he recommended walls the thickness of one and a half bricks: 'so like the feelings of men in an higher sphere are those of the poor cottager, that if his habitation be warm, cheerful and comfortable, he will return to it with gladness, and abide in it with pleasure.'

Even with cottages constructed in a material other than brick, it was the material commonly used for the chimney. Often walls of a timber-frame construction were infilled with brick, maybe replacing some earlier wall that had collapsed. Brick 'nogging' appears on some cottages, where the wall-space between the timber frame is filled with diagonally placed bricks, creating a herringbone pattern. Bricks were often combined with the local stone or flint, creating buildings with a variety of textures that were so appealing to the artists in this book.

Sir Guy Dawber, an architectural writer at the turn of the twentieth century, praised in particular the colouring on the tiles and bricks of the cottages of Kent and Sussex:

> their beauty and subtle charm: the mullioned windows and latticed frames, the tiled roofs a kaleidoscope of varied colours, the venerable walls covered with lichens, the absence of any meretricious or needless ornament, and the wonderful feeling of homeliness that pervades every feature, all combine to produce the very essence of simple and beautiful architecture.

Old cottages near Edenbridge in Kent. The timber-frame structure is hidden behind the tile-hanging. The usual practice was to nail battens onto the front of the building and then hang the tiles onto these with pegs. The joints were sometimes filled with mortar, but they were better when they simply hung free.

The clay tiles, used on the roofs and as a protective wall hanging, were particularly beautiful in the southern counties of Kent, Sussex, Surrey and Hampshire. Those hanging on the walls were thinner, but both would probably have been produced at the same time as the local bricks as they were all made in the same way. Some of the tiles were square and some were scalloped or triangular, the builders mixing the various shapes for decorative effect. On many cottages they were in all likelihood a later addition to an older finish.

Simple patterning known as pargetting appears on exterior plasterwork in the eastern counties. This too was done on top of the timber frame. The patterns were made while the plaster was wet, using a home-made implement to impress or incise simple geometric forms such as scale patterns, basketwork effects, lozenges, squares, chevrons or what was termed 'sparrow-picking', consisting of stab marks. Rarely, more elaborate patterns such scrolling foliage, flowers and birds appear on cottages in imitation of grander houses.

The composition of the plaster followed a tried and tested recipe. The main components were lime, sand and hair, with such optional additions as cow-dung or stable urine. The plaster was either white or colour-washed, and some areas were associated with particular shades, such as the buff-pink typical of Suffolk cottages. Traditionally this was limewash (lime mixed just with water), which needed to be renewed every few years as it tended to flake off. Roughcast, or 'harling' as it is generally called in Scotland, was used in many areas to add extra protection to a building. It consisted of gravel, stone chippings or coarse sand added to the plaster mixture. In Scotland shingle from the beach, including seashells, was commonly used.

Another way of providing extra warmth and protection for a timber-frame cottage was to cover it in with weather-boarding. This too was typical of the south-east: Essex, Kent and Sussex, also Hertfordshire and Buckinghamshire. Lengths of boarding were fixed horizontally onto the building, each overlapping the one below. It was a common finish for barns and mills as well as cottages. Timber-frame cottages are most in evidence in the Midlands and along the Welsh

Left: A porch constructed from rustic poles has been added to this cottage at Harvington, Worcestershire, a fashionable feature in the mid-nineteenth century.

Early nineteenth-century picturesque details: **(right).** The bargeboard and decorative timberwork on a dormer window at Alderley Edge in Cheshire.

border. This is 'black and white' country, where it was the tradition for the timbers to be accentuated with black paint and the infilling to be brightly whitewashed. No-one is clear when this fashion arose, but it is assumed that the practice became general in the seventeenth or eighteenth centuries. The original blackening would have resulted from the addition of soot or charcoal to water-based paint. Thus the plain square panelling of the post and truss structure is clearly revealed. However, the patterns made by the timber-framing occasionally became quite elaborate, with curving beams, oblique struts and now and then a quatrefoil or fleur-de-lys pierced in the beam. The pronounced gables are also frequently decorated with

Right: A typical black and white cottage among the lilac and apple blossom at Harvington in Worcestershire.

Above: A cluster of cottages round a mill in Lynmouth in Devon.

Early nineteenth-century picturesque details: **(left)** the thatched oriel lattice window on a cottage at Selworthy in Somerset.

bargeboards, some of which are likely to have been later additions.

The most characteristic image of the British cottage is perhaps represented by the combination of half-timber walls and thatched roof. The ancient word 'thack' used to mean any kind of roof covering, and we can assume that anything that came to hand was used to provide a roof over a cottage. The great advantage of thatch over stone slates was that the roof timbers could be quite light in construction. In Derbyshire flax straw was favoured, and in the Isle of Man broom, but the three most common materials were heather, straw and reed. Heather would have been used in moorland and upland areas, and it was sometimes set into a bed of clay to make it firm. Arable land provided plenty of straw from the crops of wheat, rye, oats and barley, while thatchers near wetland and coastal areas would use reed. Thatched roofs, more than any others, can merge into the landscape, seeming to appear at one with it. They also suggest a sense of warmth and comfort which is beautifully expressed in this quote from *Under the Greenwood Tree* by Thomas Hardy:

> It was a long low cottage with a hipped roof of thatch, having dormer windows breaking up into the eaves, a chimney standing in the middle of the ridge and another at each end. The window shutters were not yet closed, and the fire- and candle-light within radiated forth upon the thick bushes of box and laurestinus growing in clumps outside, and upon the bare boughs of several codlin-trees hanging about in various distorted shapes, the result of early training as espalier combined with careless climbing into their boughs in later years. The walls of the dwelling were for the most part covered with creepers, though these were rather beaten back from the doorway – a feature which was worn and scratched by much passing in and out, giving it by day the appearance of an old keyhole.

CHAPTER IV
Cottage Folk

In Miss Mitford's mind, the best place to live would be in a village, where the faces would be as familiar as the flowers in the garden; it would be:

> a little world of our own, close-packed and insulated like
> ants in an ant-hill, or bees in a hive, or sheep in a fold, or
> nuns in a convent, or sailors in a ship; where we know
> every one, are known to every one, interested in every one,
> and authorised to hope that every one feels an interest in us.

'Will you walk with me through our village', invited Miss Mitford, and, beginning at the lower end of the winding street, she described all the dwellings and their inhabitants.

In the first cottage lived a retired publican, who talked politics and read newspapers, and next to him lived the shoemaker, 'the very model of sober industry', and his pretty daughter. Opposite was the home of the village blacksmith, a man with an inveterate inclination to enter the bewitching doors of the public house; he was also the village constable, and commonly to be found in the thickest of the fray.

Outside a blacksmith's shop men would discuss market news and other matters of interest while they waited for horses to be shod and farm machinery to be repaired. The blacksmith made hoes, spades, shovels and mattocks, axes and scythes, and various other sharp-edged implements; he mended holes in pots and pans and made pattens with iron rings on the soles to keep the housewives' feet out of the mud.

Left: Myles Birket Foster's watercolour of children reading beside a country lane. The child in the middle wears a pinafore, a standard garment for Victorian children.

Week in, week out, from morn till night
You can hear his bellows blow;
You can hear him swing his heavy sledge,
With measured beat and slow,
Like a sexton ringing a village bell,
When the evening sun is low.

Left: Country people going about their daily business in the village of Biddenden, Kent. This was once an important cloth-making centre.

So wrote the poet Longfellow.

Next to the forge, in Miss Mitford's village, came the village shop:

like other village shops, multifarious as a bazaar; a repository for bread, shoes, tea, cheese, tape, ribands, and bacon; for everything, in short, except the one particular thing which you happen to want at the moment, and will be sure not to find. The people are civil and thriving, and frugal withal; they have let the upper part of the house to two young women (one of them is a pretty blue-eyed girl) who teach little children their A B C, and make caps and gowns for their mammas.

Then came a building that was 'all angles, and of a charming in-and-outness', and, close by, 'a place of importance, the Rose inn'. The landlord had 'a stirring wife, a hopeful son, and a daughter, the belle of the village . . . all curl-papers in the morning, like a porcupine, all curls in the afternoon, like a poodle, with more flounces than curl-papers, and more lovers than curls.'

In *Round about a Great Estate* Richard Jefferies gave an account of the Sun inn in the hamlet of Okebourne Wick, where, it was claimed, 'very good ale was sold':

Most of the farmers dropped in there now and then, not so much for a glass as a gossip, and no one from the

Above: Women take a moment's respite from their labours as they gossip on the doorstep. News in the village spread quickly by word of mouth.

Left: Travellers breaking their journey at a country inn. Men, women and children rest, drink, talk and dance outside this popular meeting place, while the horses, unhitched from the waggon, stand waiting patiently.

neighbouring villages or from Overboro' town ever drove past without stopping. In the 'tap' of an evening you might see the labourers playing at 'chuck-board', which consists in casting a small square piece of lead on to certain marked divisions of a shallow tray-like box placed on the trestle-table. The lead, being heavy, would stay where it fell.

'The rules I do not know,' wrote Jefferies, 'but the scene reminded me of the tric-trac contests depicted by the old Dutch painters.'

Kilvert wrote of a scene outside an inn that might have been found anywhere in Britain:

> Mr Price the Mayor was discovered in the centre of a group of village politicians before the alehouse door where
>
> 'While village statesmen talked with looks profound
> The weekly paper with their ale went round.'
>
> Tom Williams talked to the Mayor about quarrying stone for the Paincastle school while the blacksmith leaned over the wall taking part in the conversation and the rest of the village statesmen lounged in the inn porch.

On the same side of the street as the inn described by Miss Mitford lived the carpenter, his wife and their three-year-old daughter Lizzy:

> Together with a good deal of the character of Napoleon, she has something of his square, sturdy, upright form, with the finest limbs in the world, a complexion purely English, a round laughing face, sunburnt and rosy, large merry blue eyes,

curling brown hair, and a wonderful play of countenance. She has the imperial attitudes too, and loves to stand with her hands behind her, or folded over her bosom; and sometimes, when she has a little touch of shyness, she clasps them together on the top of her head, pressing down her shining curls, and looking so exquisitely pretty!

In some villages the carpenter did the work of a cooper as well, making barrels and water butts, and pails for carrying milk.

Opposite the carpenter's cottage was the collar-maker's shop, and round the corner the wheelwright's shop, essential in any rural community. The job of the

left: A farm labourer leads his horse, with a horse-drawn cart following behind him. Cottage children hung about the lanes waiting for passers-by.

Above: A waggon waits by a village inn. There was never a moment of the day when the village street was entirely empty of people.

Left: Playing on the see-saw: rough pieces of wood in the yard are used to make a plaything for the children.

Below: Two young women meet and rest at a cross marking the meeting of two lanes.

wheelwright, who often acted as the wainwright as well, was to make and repair the wheels for all the farm waggons and tradesmen's carts that were in use locally, and he was much in demand. His skill lay partly in buying the best-quality timber — mainly elm and ash, and oak for the spokes — well enough in advance to give it time to season; the prudent craftsman went so far as to lay up supplies for his son and grandson, who he supposed would follow the usual practice and succeed him in the business.

In the rope-walk at the end of the village lived the mason, one of several craftsmen employed in house building. Depending on the area and the materials that could be obtained locally, there might be a thatcher, a tiler or a plasterer living in the village, and a man who specialized in joinery as well.

Tanners and saddlers and harness-makers, carriers, who plied the roads with their horse-drawn carts loaded with goods, millers and bakers, drapers and cobblers: all had their place in village life. Jefferies told the following story when writing about village folk:

> A pig that was never a 'good doer' was found in a ditch dead. There is always a competition among the labourers for a dead pig or sheep; it was the cobbler's turn, and he had it, cut it up, and salted it down. But when in course of time he came to partake of his side of bacon, behold it was so tough and dried up that even he could not gnaw it. The side hung in the cottage for months, for he did not like to throw it away, and could not think what to do with it, for the dogs could not eat it. At last the old fellow hit upon the notion of using it as leather to mend shoes; so half his customers walked about the world on bacon heels.

Turning to walk back through the village, Miss Mitford saw two sets of cricketers on the village green. Shopkeepers and craftsmen, and ploughmen, woodsmen,

Left: In the cottages girls looked after their younger brothers and sisters as soon as their were able. A boy offers the little girl a present.

Right: 'Children love water, clear bright, sparkling water,' wrote Miss Mitford, 'it excites and feeds their curiosity; it is motion and life.'

drovers and labourers from all around, would make up enough men to play at the end of a day's work. They were surrounded by spectators, some standing, some sitting, some stretched on the grass, all taking a delighted interest in the game.

On summer evenings, Kilvert loved in his village 'to wander from cottage to cottage and from farm to farm exchanging bright words and looks with the beautiful girls at their garden gates and talking to the kindly people sitting at their cottage doors or meeting in the lane when their work is done.'

> How sweet it is to pass from house to house welcome and
> beloved everywhere by young and old, to meet the happy
> loving smiles of the dear children at their evening play in
> the lanes and fields and to meet with no harsher reproach
> than this, It is a longful while since you have been to see us.
> We do all love to see you coming.

When Kilvert went visiting in Clyro, he shared with the people of the parish all their hopes and fears, all their joys and sufferings. He saw them grow from babes in arms to lusty lads and lasses, from men and women working hard to earn a living for the family, and trying to make ends meet, to peaceful old age.

The girls helped their mothers at home 'as soon as they can waddle about', wrote William Howitt:

> They are scarcely more than infants themselves, when they
> set out to take care of other infants. The little creatures go
> lugging about great fat babies that really seem as heavy as
> themselves. You may see them on the commons, or little
> open green spots in the lanes near their homes, congregating
> together, two or three juvenile nurses, with their charges,
> carrying them along, or letting them roll in the sward, while
> they try to catch a few minutes of play with one another, or

Left: Children set out down a sandy gully typical of the Surrey countryside near Witley, watched by their mother with a baby in her arms.

with that tribe of bairns at their heels — too old to need nursing, and too young to begin nursing others.

They are often pictured a few years on wearing pinafores and pretty bonnets with kittens in their arms or feeding animals.

The games played by children in the lanes or on the green after school and in the holidays were piggy, tip-catch and hop-scotch; they skipped, played with spinning tops and bowled hoops; and they chanted 'The Three Lodgers', 'Oranges and Lemons', 'The Three Dukes', 'Old Roger' and other singing games.

A little older and the boys were to be found playing with sticks and stones, swinging on a gate, climbing trees for the excitement of it, with fishing tackle beside the brook, or paddling and splashing in the water. In winter they amused themselves breaking the ice on the ruts in the lane and sliding on a frozen pond.

The sons of labourers were put to work early on simple tasks:

to watch a gate that stands at the end of the lane or the common to stop cattle straying, and there through long solitary days they pick up a few halfpence by opening it for travellers. They are sent to scare birds from corn just sown.

They were sent out 'crow-keeping', or 'rook-scaring' of a morning as soon as it was light, armed with a pair of wooden clappers. Even after the Education Act of 1870, when parents were made responsible for seeing that their children received a proper schooling, many children missed their lessons because they were needed for field-work.

Above: 'My Rabbit' is the title given to this watercolour by Helen Allingham.

Left: Children wait with their baskets by the gate of a thatched cottage at Chiddingfold in Surrey. They were sent out to look for blackberries, mushrooms, nuts and other foods in the fields and hedges.

Another of the chores given to children was stone-picking. They collected the stones turned up by the plough in buckets and heaped them up so that they could be carted away. They often worked in gangs that included women.

At other times they might be sent out with a pair of heavy hob-nailed boots to be mended and were to be seen 'trudging along the footpaths of the fields, with the strings of the boots tied together, and slung over the shoulder — one boot behind and the other before.' And they were useful in helping to lift and carry about the farmyard: holding a sack open, shredding turnips or beetroot, bringing in wood for the fire.

At the appropriate moment in the farming year:

> They help to glean, to gather potatoes, to pop beans into holes in dibbling time, to pick hops, to gather up apples for the cider-mill, to gather mushrooms and blackberries for market, to herd flocks of geese, or young turkeys, or lambs at weaning time; they even help drive sheep to market, or to wash at shearing time.

While for the boys there were always odd jobs to be done and errands to be run out of doors, the girls made themselves useful about the cottage. The labourers' daughters:

> mop and brush, and feed the pig, and run to the town for things; and as soon as they get to ten or twelve, out they go to nurse at the farm-houses; a little older they 'go to service'; there they soon aspire to be dairymaids, or house-maids, if their ambition does not prompt them to seek places in the towns, — and so they go on scrubbing and scouring, and lending a hand in the harvest-field, till they are married to some young fellow, who takes a cottage and sets up day-labourer.

Above: A mother and her child call on an old woman on their way to the village of Wishford in Wiltshire.

Left: Childs Wickham, near Evesham, Worcestershire

Left: A harvest field on the Scottish island of Arran. 'One evening there was a small square piece cut at one side, a little notch, and two shocks stood there', wrote Richard Jefferies. 'The next day the village sent forth its army with their crooked weapons to cut and slay.'

Job, in Jefferies's *My Old Village*, was a day-labourer. He also:

> caught rats and rabbits and moles, and bought fagots or potatoes, or fruit or rabbit-skins, or rusty iron: wonderful how he seemed to have command of money. It was done probably by buying and selling almost simultaneously, so that the cash passed really from one customer to another, and was never his at all.

In his book on rural England, P. H. Ditchfield described a typical labourer's wife in later life, after she had reared a family:

> She has known what hard work meant, when she helped her husband to earn money to bring up the children by herself working in the fields. These rustic women are a fine race. They have often very tender souls in coarse bodies, wide, weather-reddened faces, not ill to look upon, calm, passive and veracious as the fields. It is hard work trimming swedes for sheep, picking up potatoes, going among the mangolds with skirts and sleeves sopping wet, the muddy soil clinging to everything.

For her, and for everyone else in the local community, harvest time was the busiest, and perhaps the happiest, time of the year. Everyday work was put aside in the villages and the woods and the fields, and the gates thrown open; the men driving horse-drawn waggons rattled along the lanes and behind them came the band of workers.

> The women leave their cottages, and are there too. Young, middle-aged, and old — all are there, to work or to glean.

Above: A girl sets out with her pail to collect milk from the farm at Ardington in Berkshire.

Left: A rural scene in Monk's Eleigh, Suffolk. The drover keeps the sheep in a well-ordered group as they pass through the village street.

The comely maiden with her rosy face, her beaming eyes, and fair figure, brings with her mirth and joke. The stout village matrons have drawn footless stockings on their arms to protect them from the sun and stubble — they have pinned up their bed-gowns behind, or doffed themselves to the brown stays and linsey-woolsey petticoat, and are amongst the best hands in the field. Even the old are feebly pulling at a rake, or putting hay into wain-row, or looking on, and telling what they have done in their time. The beer-keg is in the field, and the horn often goes round. The lunch is eaten under the tree, or amongst the sheaves.

At the end of their days in the field the men, women and children went stumbling home from the fields, the little ones, as described by Miss Mitford:

laden with bristling close-tied bunches of wheat-ears, their own gleanings, or a bottle and a basket which had contained their frugal dinner, whilst the mother would carry her babe hushing and lulling it, and the father and an elder child trudged after with the cradle, all seeming weary, and all happy.

When all was 'safely gathered in', there was a harvest supper in the barn for all the labourers. Their master feasted with them and took of the same fare — traditionally, roasted beef and mutton, plum pudding and a plentiful supply of home-brewed ale. He stood to thank them for helping with the harvest, and there were toasts to the success of farming and the prosperity of the farmer before the fiddler struck up a jolly tune, songs begun and taken up, and the tables and benches pushed back against the wall to make space for the dancing.

Harvesting at Westerham in Kent. 'No one could stand the harvest-field as a reaper except he had been born and cradled in a cottage, and passed his childhood bareheaded in July heats and January snows', Jefferies wrote.

The end to the farming year was celebrated with Harvest Festival, on a Sunday close to Michaelmas Day (September 29th). The church, specially decorated with loaves of bread baked in the form of wheat sheaves, fruit and vegetables, resounded to the people's hymns of thanksgiving and praise:

> The sower went forth sowing,
> The seed in secret slept
> Through weeks of faith and patience,
> Till out the green blade crept;
> And warm'd by golden sunshine,
> And fed by silver rain,
> At last the fields were whiten'd
> To harvest once again.
> O praise the heavenly Sower,
> Who gave the fruitful seed,
> And watch'd and water'd duly
> And ripen'd for our need.

Singing, and dancing too, were part of the wedding celebrations. On 11 November 1871 Kilvert wrote in his diary:

> This morning Catherine Price of the New Inn was married to Davies, a young Painscastle blacksmith, before the Hay registrar. What I call a gypsy 'jump the broom' marriage. The wedding feast was at the New Inn which is now shut up as an inn and abolished. As I passed the house I heard music and dancing in an upper room, unfurnished, tramp, tramp, tramp, to the jingling of a concertina, the stamping was tremendous. I thought they would have brought the floor down. They seemed to be jumping round and round. When I

Goat and kids tethered outside a cottage.

came back the dance seemed to have degenerated into a romp and the girls were squealing, as if they were being kissed or tickled and not against their will.

Apart from the festivities at Christmas, there were the mumming plays, the wassailing of the orchards, Valentine's Day, the football matches on Shrove Tuesday, the pleasant family gatherings on Mothering Sunday (the fourth Sunday in Lent), the pace-egging at Easter, the happy springtide festival of May Day, the raising of the maypole and Morris dancing, the Whitsuntide revels, wakes and rush-bearings and the bonfires on Guy Fawkes Day.

In each village the day of the revel was a special one in the calendar. As described by Ditchfield:

> it was a gladsome festival, to which all the youths and maidens looked forward for half the year and looked back on through the other half. It was the great event in the year's history which formed the general subject of conversation . . . There were horse-races, wrestling matches and merry-go-rounds, and peep-shows and menageries and waxworks, and booths and stalls for the sale of gingerbread and ribbons and laces, toys and brooches, and cocoanut 'shies' and 'all the fun of the fair.' The cheapjack, too, came with his waggon and made every one roar with laughter at his merry jokes and quaint buffoonery. Gipsies pitched their tents on the green, and the men rode in the races (gipsies are always good horsemen), or set up their cocoanuts, while the dark-skinned beauties of the tribe sold their baskets and told wondrous fortunes.

Left: High summer in the village of Bossington, near Porlock in Somerset, with a carter driving along the lane between the cottages.

Life in the villages and cottages was hard, but there were times when the toil of the daily round was put aside, and young and old joined together to make merry.

Left: In a crib by the fire a baby sleeps, with a sheepdog curled up on the cobbled floor beside it. A pelmet hangs above the fire to make it draw and keep the smoke out of the room; to the left of the hearth is a doorway leading to an upper floor.

Overleaf: 'Asleep on Duty' is the title of the painting. An old woman comes in to the cottage to find the baby crying and the girl, who is meant to be looking after him, fast asleep. On the left is a Sussex ladder-back chair, and on the shelf over the fire is a brass mortar.

CHAPTER V
Hearth and Home

'Happiness,' in William Howitt's words, 'is a fireside thing; and the simplicity of cottage life, the fewness of its objects, and the strong sympathies awakened by its trials and sufferings, tend to condense the affections, and to strike deep the roots of happiness.'

He described some of the labourers' cottages on the Duke of Northumberland's estate that were of the simplest kind: on one floor and generally with only one room:

> On one side is the fireplace, with an oven on one hand and a boiler on the other; on the opposite side of the cottage is the great partition for the beds, which are two in number, with sliding doors or curtains. The ceiling is formed by poles nailed across from one side of the roof to the other, about half a yard above where begins to slope, and covered with matting. From the matting to the wall the slope is covered with a piece of chintz in the best cottages; in others, with some showy calico print, with ordinary wall paper, or even with paper daubed with various colours and patterns.

Each had an estate number on the door and the ducal crest.

He went on to describe a cottage at the foot of the Cheviots, 'snug and curious' as were many of the shepherds' cottages thereabouts.

> This hut was of more than ordinary size, as it was required to accommodate several shepherds. The part of the house on

your left as you entered was divided into two rooms. The one was a sort of entrance lobby, where stood the cheese-press and the pails, and where hung up various shepherds' plaids, great coats, and strong shoes. In one place hung a mass of little caps with strings to them, ready to tie upon the sheeps' heads when they become galled by the fly in summer; in another were suspended wool-shears and crooks.

There was another little room, which was the dairy, 'with the oddest assemblage of wooden quaighs or little pails imaginable'.

Over these rooms, a step-ladder led to an open attic in the roof, which formed at once the sleeping apartment of the shepherds and a store-room. Here were three or four beds, some of them woollen mattresses on rude stump-bedsteads; others pieces of wicker-work, like the lower half of a pot-crate cut off, about half a yard high, filled with straw, and a few blankets laid upon it.

'There were lots of fleeces of wool stowed away,' he added, 'and lasts and awls stuck into the spars, shewed that the herds occasionally amused their leisure in winter and bad weather by cobbling their shoes.' The right-hand side of the cottage was much the same as the other, with a coved and matted ceiling, and chintz cornice, with two more beds with sliding doors.

These cottages, by comparison with some that Howitt saw around the country

Above: The simple joined stool is a piece of furniture that would have been found in many cottages. In the background is a copper used for boiling or washing, and on the wall hangs a matchet for chopping food.

A bowl of gruel is left to warm by the fire for the convalescent, who is watched over by a girl busy with her sewing. A pair of bellows hangs in the traditional place on the wall beside the fireplace.

in the 1840s, were reasonably comfortable, well maintained by the landlord and well kept by their inhabitants. Others he saw were little more than hovels. Richard Jefferies described just such a poor cottage, lived in nearly to the end of his life by a labourer:

> As a lad he went forth with his father to work in the fields, and came home to the cabbage boiled for the evening meal. It was not a very roomy or commodious home to return to after so many hours in the field, exposed to rain and wind, to snow, or summer sun. The stones of the floor were uneven, and did not fit at the edges. There was a beam across the low ceiling, to avoid which, as he grew older, he had to bow his head when crossing the apartment. A wooden ladder, or steps, not a staircase proper, behind the white-washed partition, led to the bedroom. The steps were worm-eaten and worn.

The bedroom of a cottage lived in by a large family was often divided in two by a screen, which separated the parents from their children. The big boys would sleep downstairs or were put out to sleep in the cottage of an elderly couple whose children had flown the nest.

They slept on straw pallets or in beds shared with others, perhaps lying head to toe. In some rural communities blankets were dispensed by local blanket charities and tucked in over rough sheets, and occasionally a quilt had been made of pieces of material from dresses that had been passed on to the cottagers. The poorest families had to make do with bundles of rags.

Jefferies's description continues:

> In the sitting-room the narrow panes of the small window were so overgrown with woodbine as to admit but little light. But in summer the door was wide open, and the light and the

Above: Year in year out wood had to be collected to keep the fire alight.

Left: Steam rises from the pot resting on bars across the firedogs as the child plays in her grandmother's cottage. Her other cooking utensil is a large kettle. A rough mat covers part of the brick floor.
Right: Work and play in the kitchen. Clothes hang in front of the fire to dry while a kettle is suspended on a chain over it. On the left is a ladder-back chair with a rush seat and a fine grandfather clock.

soft air came in. The thick walls and thatch kept it warm and cosy in winter when they gathered round the fire.

The fire was at the heart of cottage life. A typical cottage in early Victorian times had in the main room a large, wide fireplace and inglenook opposite the door, with a larder on one side and a staircase leading to an upper floor on the other. A beam ran across the top of the fireplace, with a short curtain to keep the smoke away from the room. Until ranges were installed in the cottages, beginning in the 1880s, the food was usually cooked in an iron pot suspended from a hook over an open fire, and from the same hook were hung a kettle and the occasional joint of meat for roasting. In some cottages the cooking pot was supported on bars that

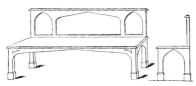

Left: A fisherman's cottage with the kettle boiling on a grate.

Below: The dresser was the principal piece of cottage furniture, used for the storage and the display of all the household china: everything, from the teapot to the earthenware jars for pickling and preserving, were to be found on its shelves.

rested on either side of a wood fire on iron firedogs, which were designed to increase the draught to the flame. The fire was kept burning all the time, with beside it a load of sticks collected from the woods and lanes.

The main room was truly the 'living-room' for it was here that a woman spent almost all her days, with her children about her feet or in a crib at the fireside, and a man the few hours between work and sleep.

In the lowliest dwellings, in Howitt's description, the room was very sparsely furnished:

> A few chairs, a deal table, three or four shelves, and a cupboard, with a box or two in the corners, constitute the whole. The domestic utensils are few, and strictly utilitarian. A great pot, a kettle, a saucepan, a few plates, dishes and knives, half-a-dozen spoons, and that is about all. But on the mantelpiece there is nearly sure to be a few ornaments in crockery, bought from some itinerant trader.

John Claudius Loudon considered a dresser to be an essential piece of furniture in every cottage, but by no means all households could afford one. 'They are generally made by joiners, and seldom painted, it being the pride of good housewives, in most parts of England, to keep the boards of which they are composed as white as snow by frequently scouring them with fine white sand.' On it were displayed cups and saucers, traditionally willow pattern, and perhaps a fine china teapot, a present from the 'big house' when a servant left service to be married. 'You must be prepared to see her take out of it, before the tea is made, a packet of snuff, two or three cough-lozenges that have seen better days, a packet of needles, and a few other unconsidered trifles,' wrote P. H. Ditchfield.

Settles were to be found in some cottages, while a valued possession was a grandfather clock, handed on from one generation to the next: 'It has only one hand, and has to be wound up every night; and the interior cogwheels are not

Above: A view of the sea from the window of a fisherman's home. In some villages it was traditional for the women to stay indoors until the fishing boats had come in and their menfolk had returned to them.

Left: Geraniums in pots in a cottage window. The clock is hung high on the wall to allow the weights a reasonable drop. Other items on the walls include a picture of Queen Victoria and a page from *The Churchman's Almanac*.

very evenly cut, so that some hours pass more rapidly than others.' Articles made of pewter were also much treasured.

On the walls might be found a sampler, cuttings from pictorial papers, including one of Queen Victoria and, from the 1860s, a portrait photograph, taken by a travelling photographer or in the local town. A family where the men worked as carters might display relics of their working life: 'two or three sets of brightly polished brass ornaments which were used for decorating horses and were fastened on the strap that connects the collar with the belly-band.' They came in various forms, some crescent shaped, others with pierced decoration of a crown or a star. Other keepsakes were, in a farming community, old farm implements and, in a fishing community, nets and objects collected on the shore. And old rushlight and candle holders were often kept, even after the cottages were lit with oil lamps.

There was no doubt that flowers added cheer to a room. Kilvert, after paying a visit to the cottage of old Richard Clark and his pretty young wife ('lately Edward Morgan's concubine'), wrote:

> I had thought Edward Morgan had a comfortless, miserable home. I was never more mistaken or surprised. The cottage was exquisitely clean and neat, with a bright blue cheerful paper and almost prettily furnished. A vase of bright fresh flowers stood upon each table and I could have eaten my dinner off every stone of the floor. The girl said no one ever came near the house to see it, and she kept it for her own satisfaction. The oven door was screened from view by a little curtain and everything was made the most and best of. I don't wonder Morgan married the girl.

Rag rugs on the flagstones or earth floor also added colour, and brightly coloured cushions made from scraps of material.

Turning to the manner in which they were sustained, the mass of cottagers lived on bread, bacon, lard and weak tea as their staple diet, and whatever fruit and vegetables they could grow themselves. Eggs and milk were available to many, and, according to the season, they were able to gather blackberries from the hedgerows, watercress from the streams, hazel nuts, chestnuts and crab apples. Workers on the land were often able to bring home rabbits and pigeons.

William Cobbett, in his zeal to better the lot of 'the labouring classes of this kingdom', produced a book entitled *Cottage Economy*, in which he attempted to show them how best to manage their affairs. He laid down as a maxim that 'for a family to be happy, they must be well supplied with food and raiment', and proceeded to offer his advice. In the first chapter, on beer and brewing, he advocated that the labourer's wife should brew beer instead of making tea: 'It must be evident to every one, that the practice of tea drinking must render the frame feeble and unfit to encounter hard labour or severe weather;' from tea-drinking follows 'a softness, an effeminacy, a seeking for the fireside, a lurking in the bed, and, in short, all the characteristics of idleness.'

Home-brewed beer kept the men away from the public houses while the tea provided in most cottages made the frequenting of them habitual. Furthermore, tea:

> corrupts boys as soon as they are able to move from home, and does little less for the girls, to whom the gossip of the tea-table is no bad preparatory school for the brothel. At the very least, it teaches them idleness. The everlasting dawdling about with the slops of the tea-tackle gives them a relish for nothing that requires strength and activity. When they go from home, they know how to do nothing that is useful. To brew, to bake, to make butter, to milk, to rear poultry.

From brewing beer, Cobbett moved on to baking bread, and again he recommended that this should be done at home. Fuel to heat the oven was easily

Above: From a cottage at Charlton King's in Gloucestershire a woman sets out with her basket.

Left: Near Freshwater, on the Isle of Wight, a woman glances at her ducks as she walks home with a pail. Poultry was generally the concern of the women.

found, and at no cost. In his opinion bread made from rye and barley as well as wheat was more wholesome than the baker's wheat loaf.

Keeping cows was his next subject, and he advised on their feed and the breed of animal suited to the quality and quantity of the grazing. Then comes his chapter on keeping pigs. 'A couple of flitches of bacon are worth fifty thousand Methodist sermons and religious tracts', he wrote. 'The sight them upon the rack tends more to keep a man from poaching and stealing than whole volumes of penal statutes.' In all, 'They are great softeners of the temper, and promoters of domestic harmony'.

A pig was kept by every cottage family with the means to do so, for every part of the animal could be used to feed hungry mouths. Even the offal could be made to last a large family for a week, with hog's pudding for the children and some for the neighbours' children too. The butcher returned the day after he had been called in to kill the pig to cut up the carcass. 'Souse, griskins, blade-bones, thigh-bones, spare-ribs, chines, belly-pieces, cheeks': all provided meat for the household for another four or five weeks, and the rest was cured for bacon.

All manner of fowl, goats and ewes, were commented on by Cobbett, and then he turned his readers' attention to 'the converting of English Grass, and Grain Plants, cut green, into Straw, for the purpose of making Plat for Hats and Bonnets.' It seemed to him that the cutting, bleaching, sorting and plaiting of straw was of all employments the best suited to the wives and children of country labourers. In *Rural Rides* he described having seen an instance of this home industry:

> I was very much pleased with what I saw at Durley, which is about two miles from Botley, and is certainly one of the most obscure villages in this whole kingdom. Mrs Mears, the farmer's wife, had made, of the crested dog's tail grass, a bonnet which she wears herself. I there saw girls platting the straw. They had made plat of several degrees of fineness; and, they sell it to some person or persons at Fareham, who, I suppose, makes it into bonnets.

Left: Taking a moment's rest from her work as a seamstress, a woman dozes at her worktable. She is watched by a child who has returned from school and hung her slate on the back of the chair.

Above: At the Old Tucking Mill, Bridport, Dorset. Geese were raised by grazing, but to fatten them they were fed corn, turnips and carrots, cabbages and gone-to-seed lettuces from the garden.

Left: An everyday scene outside a cottage on a sunny day. The woman is using her apron to carry items that she has gathered.

Mrs Mears had two girls at work, each of them earning in a week almost as much as their father, who was a labourer:

> These two girls (and not very stout girls) earn six shillings a week each: thus the income of this family is, from seven shillings a week, raised to nineteen shillings a week. I shall suppose that this may in some measure be owing to the generosity of the ladies in the neighbourhood, and to their desire to promote this domestic manufacture . . . Very little, indeed, could these poor things have done in the field during the last forty days.

As many women and children as were engaged in strawplaiting were employed in lacemaking. It was an occupation requiring greater skill, and from the age of five or six children were sent to lace schools to learn the craft. The main centres of the industry were Devon, Oxfordshire, Northamptonshire, Buckinghamshire and Bedfordshire. During the day the workers sat in the window of their cottages, or at the door, so as to catch the best light. Across their knees or on a stool was the hard round pillow with the design in horn parchment laid flat upon it.

> Yon cottager, who weaves at her own door
> Pillow and bobbins, all her little store;
> Content, though mean, and cheerful, if not gay,
> Shuffling her threads about the livelong day

In the evenings they struggled to see by candlelight, using bottles filled with water to magnify the beam.

Kilvert, on his walks through his Radnorshire parish, saw several women at their work. He wrote in his diary:

Top: A doorstep discussion 'At Granny's'.

Above: Knitting at the door of a cottage near Oxford.

Left: Teatime outside the cottage on a fine summer's day.

Old Hannah Whitney was sitting in her cottage door at work as usual with her high cap and her little red shawl pinned over her breast, her thin grey-bearded nutcracker face bent earnestly upon her knitting till she glanced sharply up over her spectacles to see who it was that was passing.

'The old folks used to rise very early, never later than five even in winter,' he commented, 'and then the women would get to their spinning or knitting.' They had their breakfast just before daylight in winter, and 9 o'clock at night was a very late hour for going to bed. 'When people rose early it was a saying that they were "beating for day", because it was supposed that they went out and knocked on the earth for day to come.'

In the Dales, where the women seemed to knit incessantly, Howitt observed some curious practices. In the evening, after the children had been put to bed, the women of the neighbourhood assembled in one of the cottages:

They sit rocking to and fro like so many weird wizards. They burn no candle, but knit by the light of the peat fire. And this rocking motion is connected with a mode of knitting peculiar to the place, called swaving, which is difficult to describe. Ordinary knitting is performed by a variety of little motions, but this is a single uniform tossing motion of both the hands at once, and the body often accompanying it with a sort of sympathetic action . . . They knit with crooked pins called pricks; and use a knitting-sheath of a dagger, curved to the side, and fixed in a belt called the cowband.

Women knitted stockings and jackets for their families, and made other garments from linen, cotton and woollen cloth. The cottagers wore clothes that were

Above: A woman looks dreamily out of the window as she stays indoors to mind the baby. A window seat has been made in the thickness of the cottage walls.

Left: The bundle of washing leaving a cottage at Bruton Bradstock in Somerset. Many cottagers took in washing for a living.

Right: Returning home with the rhubarb for making tarts and pies.

sometimes made less of a single length of material than of an assemblage of different scraps.

Young women, the wives of labourers, were usually employed for part of the year out of doors, weeding and collecting stones from the fields, hop-picking and harvesting. Every day they looked after their children, cooked and washed — some of them took in washing for a living — fed the cow and the pig, the chickens and the geese, went looking for firewood and brought home mushrooms, blackberries and anything else to be found in the fields and hedgerows.

Passing by Mrs Martin's cottage one day, Kilvert found her engaged in a singular occupation:

She was busy picking pheasants' feathers to make a pillow. Talking of feather beds she said, 'Pheasants' feathers will do very well for a bed, but not pigeons' feathers. People don't like to sleep on pigeons' feathers.' 'Why not?' I asked. 'Well,' said Susan Martin mysteriously, 'folk do say that a person can't die on pigeons' feathers.'

CHAPTER VI
Cottage Gardens

The English poet John Clare was born in 1793 in the village of Helpstone in Northamptonshire, the son of a poor labourer. One of his most famous poems, *Proposals for Building a Cottage*, has few instructions for the cottage itself, beyond that 'The door may open with a string, so that it closes tight', and that it be positioned beside a stream with 'broad oaks o'er its chimney spread'. However the proposals for the garden run to several verses and express the particular atmosphere of peace and happiness that the idea of the simple cottage garden evokes:

> A little garden, not too fine,
> Inclose with painted pales;
> And woodbines, round the cot to twine,
> Pin to the wall with nails.
>
> Let hazels grow, and spindling sedge,
> Bent bowering overhead;
> Dig old man's beard from woodland hedge,
> To twine the summer shade.
>
> Beside the threshold sods provide,
> And build a summer seat;
> Plant sweetbrier bushes by its side,
> And flowers that blossom sweet.

Left: A girl draws water from her well for the pansies that grow beside the path. Clover and ox-eye daisies can be seen growing among the meadow grass in front of her cottage.

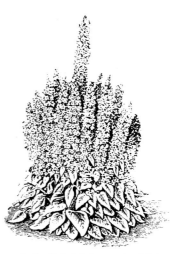

Left: Delphiniums rise high above the hedge of this fine timber-framed cottage, with rambling roses intertwined in the hedge.

Right: Massed flowers provide a riot of colour, with the tall hollyhock as the backdrop: the very essence of a cottage garden.

I love the sparrow's ways to watch
Upon the cotters' sheds,
So here and there pull out the thatch,
That they may hide their heads.

And as the sweeping swallows stop
Their flights along the green,
Leave holes within the chimney-top
To paste their nest between.

Most cottage gardens would have included plants brought in from the wild.
'Dig old man's beard', Clare wrote. Dorothy Wordsworth, sister of the poet,
described in her journal the creation of their shared garden at Dove Cottage at
Grasmere, and how she transplanted snowdrops, primroses, wild strawberries,
foxgloves, orchids and columbines collected during her walks in the
countryside. In a letter to a friend she wrote happily about her garden:

> We have . . . a small orchard and a smaller garden which
> as it is the work of our own hands we regard with pride
> and partiality . . . Our cottage is quite large enough for us
> though very small, and we have made it neat and
> comfortable within doors, and it looks very nice on the
> outside, for though the roses and the honeysuckles which
> we have planted against it are only of this year's growth
> yet it is covered all over with green leaves and scarlet
> flowers, for we have trained scarlet beans upon threads,
> which are not only exceedingly beautiful, but very useful,
> as their produce is immense.

The Wordsworths when they moved to Dove Cottage were certainly poorly off,

Above: A country boy feeds turnip tops to his rabbits. Nothing in cottage life was wasted.

Left: The garden of a stone and thatched cottage at Crewkerne, Somerset, in spring. Tulips, pansies, wallflowers and forget-me-nots edge the path, while cabbages and currant bushes are grown behind them.

and Dorothy's enthusiasm for her beans underlines one of the prime purposes of the cottage garden, which was to augment the family supply of food.

John Clare's origins were humble but his vision of the cottage garden was widely appreciated by people of all classes, who felt that its simple charm was a beacon of goodness in a changing world. Stewart Dick in The *Cottage Homes of England* wrote in 1909 that cottagers have 'been least touched by the industrial changes which have made the modern commercial world.'

> After all in spite of patent self-binding machines and steam-threshers, the alternation of seed-time and harvest is just the same as ever it was. It is the same good brown earth that brings forth its fatness; they plough the same fields that their grandfathers ploughed before them. The same landscape meets their eyes, the same river flows down by the mill . . . And so it is with special pride that the cottager clings to his garden. Away back in the past his forefathers owned in a sort of way their own little strips of the common land, and now this is all that is left to him. Still, such as it is, it is his own, and his labour there is truly a labour of love.

The labour of love and leisure is described in another of Clare's poems, *A Cottage Garden:*

> Where rustic taste a leisure trimly weaves
> The rose and straggling woodbine to the eaves,
> And on the crowded spot that pales enclose
> The white and scarlet daisy rears in rows,
> Training the trailing peas in clusters neat,
> Perfuming the evening with a luscious sweet —

And sunflowers planting for their gilded show
That scale the window's lattice ere they blow,
And seen to cottagers within the sheds,
Peep through the crystal panes their golden heads.

During the Victorian period gardening became a very elaborate and labour-intensive science: the fashion was forhothouses growing exotic fruits and plants from all around the world, and for intricately patterned flowerbeds densely planted with brightly-coloured annuals. The cottage garden was the antithesis of this: a picturesque profusion combining rows of vegetables, beehives, fruit trees and poultry with richly-scented old-fashioned flowers and creepers. Gardening was seen as a particularly worthwhile pastime, encouraging all the best virtues of thrift, productivity and healthy activity. A poem by Mary Howitt speculates on the contentment engendered by the perfect cottage garden:

Around the rich man's trellised bower
Gay, costly creepers run:
The poor man has his scarlet-beans
To screen him from the sun.

And there before the little bench
O'ershadowed by the bower,
Grow southernwood and lemon-thyme
Sweet-pea and gillyflower;

And here on sabbath evenings,
Until the stars are out,
With little one either hand,
He walketh all about.

Above: A woman stands on the paved path leading to her cottage door, the flowers in the garden in full bloom.

Left: The summer glory of peonies and of pinks, grown especially for their scent, greet the woman as she makes her way through the garden to hang out her washing.

Above: A girl walks to church in her Sunday best on a path bordered with lilac.

Left: Chickens peck in the rough grass beneath the old orchard trees beside this cottage.

For though his garden plot is small,
Him doth it satisfy;
For there's no inch of all his ground
That does not fill his eye.

No corner of the plot was wasted in the cottage garden, and there was certainly no place for an unproductive lawn. The average extent was about one-eighth to one-quarter of an acre. In an early manual for cottage gardeners, John Claudius Loudon suggested that one-eighth of an acre (or twenty rods) was plenty to provide vegetables for a family of five, and listed onions, leeks, carrots, beans, parsnips, cabbages, runner beans and potatoes as suitable crops, with radishes, peas, lettuce and cucumber, and tobacco, as possible additions if space allowed. He also reckoned that a pig and some fowls could be kept in a garden this size. If the garden was larger, or in an allotment, some barley might be grown for the pig. William Cobbett stated in his book *Cottage Economy* that 'The cottager's pig should be bought in the spring or late in winter; and being then four months old, he will be a year before killing time; for, it should always be borne in mind, that this age is required in order to insure the greatest quantity of meat from a given quantity of food.'

Depending on the shape of the garden, vegetables were traditionally grown at the back of the cottage and flowers were grown in the front, in particular along the front paling or wall and edging the path that led up to the door. The gardener Gertrude Jekyll, who had a keen appreciation of the cottage gardens near where she lived in Surrey, described how 'The Pinks and Wall-flowers, Pansies and Sweet-Williams of the cottage flower-borders never look so well as when hanging over the edges of these paved paths.' While in Surrey the paths noted by Jekyll were of local sandstone and odd bricks, a variety of materials elsewhere were used in an attempt, no doubt, to keep the mud at bay in winter. Another writer noted that she had seen oyster shells, and even an edging of shank-bones from sheep. Perhaps these were a variation on Mary, Mary, Quite Contrary's cockle shells.

Gertrude Jekyll gave further descriptions of the cottage front gardens in her book *Old West Surrey,* which she wrote in 1904.

> Cottage folk are great lovers of flowers, and their charming little gardens in villages and by the roadside, are some of the most delightful incidents of road-travel in our southern counties . . . If the space is a small one it is often all given to flowers. Sometimes, indeed, the smaller the space the more is crammed into it. One tiny garden, that I used to watch with much pleasure, had nearly the whole space between road and cottage filled with a rough staging. It was a good example of how much could be done with little means but with much loving labour . . . There were hydrangeas, fuchsias, show and zonal geraniums, lilies and begonias . . . a clematis smothered in bloom, over the door . . . it must have given pleasure to thousands of passers-by.

Left: Chickens and ducks roamed freely in the cottagers' gardens, their eggs providing a welcome addition the everyday fare.

From this description it is clear that, despite the fence or wall, the boundary between the cottage and the track or road on which it was built was often indistinct. Children could play beside the road undisturbed and untroubled.

It was certainly important for most of the plants to earn their keep in the garden, and besides those grown for food there would have been herbs for a multitude of uses. In *Lark Rise to Candleford,* Flora Thompson described the herb patch as having 'thyme and parsley and sage for cooking, rosemary to flavour the home-made lard, lavender to scent the best clothes and peppermint, pennyroyal, horehound, camomile, tansy, balm and rue for physic.' Herbs listed by Richard Jefferies include southernwood and mugwort. Many herbs and plants were made into 'teas', or infusions, specifics for different maladies or conditions: thus raspberry-leaf for reducing pain in childbirth, limeflower

for breathing difficulties, and dandelion and honey tea for biliousness. The soporific properties of the hop were also well known. Rhubarb, the use of which was originally purely medicinal, only gradually became popular as a filling for pies and tarts.

Many plants were loved for their fragrance and were often hung in bunches to sweeten the linen and scent the air, especially sweet woodruff and meadowsweet. Plants were also grown for their qualities as insect-repellants; the violet was used against fleas, while lavender deterred moth. Flora Thompson's choice does not vary much from one that John Clare made in a poem called *Flowers in my Time*, and perhaps the presence of the marigold was for companion planting with cabbage to protect it against whitefly.

> And where the marjoram once, and sage and rue,
> And balm and mint, with curled-leaf parsley grew,
> And double marigolds, and silver thyme,
> And pumpkins 'neath the window used to climb;
> And where I often, when a child, for hours
> Tried through the pales to get the tempting flowers;
> As lady's laces, everlasting peas,
> True-love lies bleeding, with the hearts at ease;
> And golden rods, and tansy running high,
> That o'er the pale-top smiled on passer-by;
> Flowers in my time which every one would praise . . .

Above: Gazing out at the garden on a fine summer's day.

Left: A cottage in springtime: the bees, according to the practice of the day, were put in hives with fresh straw, and these were placed on a bench to keep them safe from mice. The broken crocks on top were to prevent their getting wet.

A HERITAGE OF COUNTRY LIFE

Many of the flowers and the blossom in cottage gardens provided bees with nectar and pollen: the fruit trees in spring, mignonette, borage, thyme, clover, golden rod, hyssop and lavender, as well as bean and pea flowers. Not only were bees recognized for their valuable work in pollinating the fruit trees but also for providing useful beeswax and glorious golden honey at the summer's end.

In many paintings of cottage gardens there is a row of woven straw bee-skeps. Mead, a powerful drink made from fermented honey, may have been one of the attractions of beekeeping. The writer George Borrow, who described his country travels in a book called *Romany Rye,* was invited to drink mead by an old man he met on the road. They went to his 'very pretty cottage, delightfully situated within a garden, surrounded by a hedge of woodbines', and into his cottage, where:

> making me sit down by a deal table in a neatly sanded kitchen, he produced from an old-fashioned closet a bottle, holding about a quart, and a couple of cups, which might each contain about half a pint, then opening the bottle and filling the cups with a brown-coloured liquor, he handed one to me, and taking a seat opposite to me, he lifted the other, nodded, and saying to me 'Health and welcome,' placed it to his lips and drank. 'Health and thanks,' I replied; and being very thirsty, emptied my cup at a draught; I had scarcely done so, however, when I half repented. The mead was deliciously sweet and mellow, but appeared as strong as brandy; my eyes reeled in my head, and my brain became slightly dizzy.

George Borrow was later shown the old man's beehives:

As can be seen from these pictures, the peacock was seen as a particularly challenging topiary creation. A. R. Quinton painted the one at Norton, near Evesham in Worcestershire (left), and Helen Allingham the one at West Horsley, Surrey (far left).

Gardeners made full use of cottage and garden walls for growing creepers or training fruit trees, such as pears. These cottages were painted by Helen Allingham at Shere in Surrey (left) and on the Isle of Wight (right).

In the garden was the habitation of the bees, a long box, supported upon three oaken stumps. It was full of small round glass windows, and appeared to be divided into a great many compartments, much resembling drawers placed sideways. He told me that, as one compartment was filled, the bees left it for another; so that, whenever he wanted honey, he could procure some without injuring the insects. Through the little round windows I could see several of the bees at work; hundreds going in and out of the door; hundreds were buzzing about on the flowers, the woodbines and the beans. As I looked around on the well-cultivated field, the garden and the bees, I thought I had never seen so rural and peaceful a scene.

Fruit trees were likely to be grown round the margins of the garden, or trained against the southern wall of the cottage, where the sun-warmed walls would hasten the ripening of the fruit. Apples, pears, damsons and plums, and maybe a quince or a bullace tree, were all favoured. When there was a particularly abundant harvest, the surplus fruit might be sold by the cottager at market. In a spare corner of the garden there might also be room for a few stands of hazel, which could be coppiced for pea-sticks and which would provide nuts in autumn. Much could be gathered from the hedgerows and did not need to be cultivated in the garden: blackberries, filberts and wild flowers such as daffodils, snowdrops and violets, which were often gathered by cottage children to sell. Currant and gooseberry bushes were very popular, gooseberries being especially prized and loved, far more than strawberries.

An old woman in here autumn garden with michaelmas daisies mingling with fully-grown cabbages.

Late summer flowers in a Dorset front garden

Topiary, as can be seen in several of these paintings, was also a beloved feature of cottage gardens. Perhaps some of the creators of these ingeniously trimmed creations worked as gardeners in the nearby great houses, since topiary was also extremely fashionable in large Victorian formal gardens, imparting a sense of antiquity, or so their owners thought. In the North a rowan tree was often planted at the gate in order to bring good fortune.

For flowers the cottage gardener was unlikely to have spare money to buy seeds or plants, so he would carefully collect seed from one year to the next, and propagate new plants from cuttings. The range of flowers was therefore limited, and probably remained unchanged for many generations. Among the most prominent flowers was what one writer called 'the towering splendour of the hollyhocks'; they were introduced to Britain in the sixteenth century and were only equalled in size and colour by the sunflowers. The white and fragrant cottage lily, introduced to this country from the East during the Middle Ages, can often be spotted, its scent mingling with that of the gillyflower or clove-scented pink.

Nasturtiums, stocks, larkspurs, phlox were other summer favourites, with primroses, auriculas, lilies-of-the-valley and forget-me-nots in spring. The sweet-scented honeysuckle (or woodbine as it was also called) was the archetypical climber, often intermingling with old-fashioned climbing roses. The scent of the sweetbriar was much loved, and Gertrude Jekyll introduced it into her own garden: 'There are balmy days in mid-April, when the whole garden is fragrant with Sweetbriar. It is not "fast of its smell" as Bacon says of the damask rose, but gives it so lavishly that one cannot pass near a plant without being aware of its gracious presence.'

ALLINGHAM, Helen (1848-1926)

Born in Derbyshire, the daughter of a doctor, she spent most of her early life in Birmingham. In 1867 she was accepted into the Royal Academy Schools in London. In 1874 she married the poet William Allingham, and in 1881 they went to live at Sandhills, near Witley in Surrey. Her neighbour there was Myles Birket Foster (*q.v.*). She found in the neighbourhood the subject that was to engage her interest for the rest of her life: the cottages and homesteads of England. Her watercolours are illustrated in *Cottage Homes of England* by Stewart Dick and *Happy England*, a biography of the artist, by Marcus Huish.

CLARE, John (1793-1864)

The son of a Northamptonshire labourer, he produced some of the most artless and appealing rural poetry in the English language. He published *Poems Descriptive of Rural Life and Scenery* in 1820, *The Village Minstrel* in 1821, *The Shepherd's Calendar* in 1827 and *The Rural Muse* in 1835. Soon after this he began to suffer from a disturbance of the mind and was committed to an asylum, where he continued to write poetry

COBBETT, William (1763-1835)

The son of a farmer in Surrey, he was involved for most of his life in political matters, first as a journalist and later as an M.P. In 1792 he went to live in America to avoid prosecution after he had accused officers with whom he had served in the army of embezzlement. There he published pro-British pamphlets under the name 'Peter Porcupine'. On his return to England he founded *Cobbett's Political Register*. Querulous by nature and independent in his views, he was imprisoned for two years for his attack on flogging in the army. He later took up the cause of parliamentary reform. His observations on living conditions in various parts of England were written on a tour of the country on horseback; they were published as articles in his *Register* and in book form in 1830 as *Rural Rides*. *Cottage Economy*, 'deemed useful in the conducting of the affairs of a Labourer's Family' was published in 1821.

FOSTER, Myles Birket (1825-99)

Born in Northumberland into an old north-country Quaker family, he was sent to London in 1841 as an apprentice to the wood-engraver Ebenezer Landells. The first of his illustrations for *Punch* was published in that year. He later worked as a draughtsman for the *Illustrated London News* and illustrated the works of Milton, Scott and Wordsworth. In 1859 he turned from engraving to painting, working mainly in watercolours. His favourite subjects were Surrey landscapes with figures by the roadside or in woodland, the small-scale scenes carefully composed and meticulously finished.

HOWITT, Mary (1799-1888)

The daughter of a prosperous Quaker from Staffordshire, she read widely as a child and soon began to write poetry. In 1821 she married William Howitt (*q.v.*) and together they contributed pieces — mainly in verse — to various periodicals. Her own reputation rests on her stories for children and books on natural history. While living in Heidelberg in 1840 she studied Swedish and Danish, and afterwards translated Hans Andersen's tales into English. 'William and Mary', as they were called on account of their various combined efforts, were admired for their amiability and for their industry in 'spreading good and innocent literature'.

HOWITT, William (1792-1879)

A writer, linguist and at one time practising spiritualist, he was a man with diverse interests, and a truly Victorian thirst for knowledge and desire for self-improvement. He propounded on a wide variety of subjects, the titles of his books ranging from *The History of the Supernatural in all Ages and Nations* (1863) to *The Religion of Rome* (1873), from *Homes and Haunts of the most eminent British Poets* (1847) to *The Student Life of Germany*, the latter written while living in Heidelberg for the benefit of his children's education. His most popular books on England and life in the country, included *Rural Life of England* (1838) and *The Hall and the Hamlet* (1848). After travelling in Australia, and working in a gold-field, he wrote several books on that country. In 1870 he settled in Rome, where he became involved in the formation of a society for the protection of animals and a project for planting *Eucalyptus globulus*, which was recognized for its usefulness in the fight against malaria. He died in Rome.

JEFFERIES, Richard (1848-87)

The son of a Wiltshire farmer, he attempted at the age of sixteen to run away to Moscow, changing his destination to America before giving up and returning home. He became a reporter on local news-papers and wrote several unsuccessful novels before *The Gamekeeper at Home* was published in 1877. This marked the beginning of his popularity as an author. He is known especially for his acute powers of observation and almost poetic sensitivity in describing nature and the English countryside. He wrote of himself, 'Never was such a worshipper of earth. The commonest pebble, dusty and marked with the stain of the ground, seems to me so wonderful; my mind works round it till it becomes the sun and centre of a system of thought and feeling.'

KILVERT, Francis (1840-79)

For many years curate of Langley Burrell in Radnorshire, he kept a diary from 1870 onwards. It is an affectionate record of the commonplaces of life, set mainly in the Welsh borders. As he went about his duties on foot, he delighted in the scenery and in his friendship with parishioners.

QUINTON, Alfred Robert (*fl.* 1853-1907)

Trained as a painter at Heatherley's art school in London, his talent was as a painter of landscapes, in which he captured the essential spirit of country life in late Victorian and Edwardian England. He illustrated books on the Wye Valley and Wharfdale and P. H. Ditchfield's *Rural England* .

WHITE, Gilbert (1720-93)

He was born and spent almost all his life in the Hampshire village of Selborne. He was deeply attached to the neighbourhood and from 1751, while carrying out his duties as curate, he kept detailed records of the seasonal changes to the landscape and to the habits of wild animals. His correspondence with two distinguished naturalists formed the basis of his *Natural History and Antiquities of Selborne*, which was published in 1767.

WORDSWORTH, Dorothy (1771-1855)

She was the sister of William Wordsworth and his constant companion. The journal that she kept at Grasmere in the Lake District, between 1800 and 1803, includes interesting descriptions of the countryside and of the lives of local people as well as everyday life at Dove Cottage. Some of the entries relate directly to passages in William's poems.

BIBLIOGRAPHY

Sidney Oldall Addy *The Evolution of the English House*, 1933

S. Baring-Gould *An Old English Home*, 1898

Harry Batsford and Charles Fry *The English Cottage*, 1938

Alec Clifton-Taylor *The Pattern of English Building*, 1972

William Cobbett *Cottage Economy*, 1822

Gillian Darley *Villages of Vision*, 1974

W. G. Davie *Old Cottages in the Cotswold District*, 1905

W. G. Davie *Old Cottages in Kent and Sussex*, 1900

W. G. Davie *Old Cottages in Surrey*, 1908

Stewart Dick *The Cottage Homes of England*, 1909

P. H. Ditchfield *Rural Life in England*, 1912

W. D. Drury *The Book of Gardening*, 1900

Pamela Horn *Labouring Life in the Victorian Countryside*, 1976

William Howitt *The Rural Life in England*, 1840

Marcus Huish *Happy England*, 1909

C. F. Innocent *The Development of English Building Construction*, 1916

Richard Jefferies *Field and Hedgerow*, 1892

Richard Jefferies *The Life of the Fields*, 1888

Sydney R. Jones *English Village Homes*, 1936

Graham Nicholson and Jane Fawcett *The Village in History*, 1988

Anne Scott-James *The Cottage Garden*, 1981

David Souden *The Victorian Village*, 1991

Adrian Tinniswood *Life in the English Country Cottage*, 1995

ACKNOWLEDGEMENTS

The illustrations on the following pages are by A. R. Quinton, and are reproduced by kind courtesy of The Salmon Studio, Sevenoaks, Kent: 16, 17, 20, 32, 46, 48, 56, 63, 64, 76 (left), 78, 86, 87, 88, 92, 106, 110, 111, 114, 152 (right) and 156 (right). Christie's Images of Langley Lane, London SW8 1TH supplied the following: front and back cover, 10, 12, 18, 21, 24, 26, 27, 28, 34, 36, 38, 39, 41, 42, 43, 45, 53, 54, 58, 60, 62, 68, 70, 72, 74, 81, 89, 90, 94, 95, 96, 98, 97, 99, 100, 101, 104, 108, 113, 115, 118, 119, 120, 122, 123, 124, 125, 126, 127, 130, 132, 134, 137, 143, 145, 146, 147, 148, 151 and 154.